About the author

C. T. Sullivan is a singer-songwriter and stand-up comedian. He is also the author of the much-acclaimed crime thriller *Reasonable Force* (Pegasus Publishers).

Having recently retired as a city money-broker, he went to live in Manhattan for three months with his wife Deborah when she was seconded to her New York office. There, purely as ballast, he kept a journal of his experiences and observations whilst delving down into the colourful history of this iconic city.

After a one year move from Surrey to Devon, he now lives in Sussex with his wife, Deborah, and Labrador, Woof.

Author's Website: ctsullivan.co.uk

APPLE INSIDER

C. T. Sullivan

APPLE INSIDER

Vanguard Press

A CIP catalogue record for this title is
available from the British Library.

ISBN 978 1 784653 57 6

Vanguard Press is an imprint of
Pegasus Elliot MacKenzie Publishers Ltd.
www.pegasuspublishers.com

First Published in 2018

Vanguard Press
Sheraton House Castle Park
Cambridge England

Printed & Bound in Great Britain

Dedication

To my patient, clever and loving wife, Deborah.

To Mason Mount (Chelsea academy player) and parents Tony and Debbie for the trust, joy, and one of the most fulfilling times in my life. Good luck in your career, Mason.

To Maureen Druce for being so delightful and supportive in everything that I do.

Acknowledgements

Thanks to Susan Davis for her time, invaluable input and support.

Chapter One

'Three months. Thirteen weeks to be precise.'

These were the two short sentences my wife's boss delivered across the exquisitely laid table in a packed Simpson's-in-the-Strand. As the keen but courtly wine waiter charged our half-full glasses I turned to my wife, Deb. Two sets of eyebrows lifted in perfect unison. Those seven words, issued within the nut-brown oak-panelled walls of this cherished canteen were exhilarating and scary in equal measure. But they were the green light to ninety-one days of surprises, frustrations, joy and much craziness. Deb was needed in her New York office. This was to be our Manhattan adventure.

I've always had a sneaky suspicion that Frank Sinatra was not the first to start spreading the news; but spread it he did. Not only were we informed that this city was so good they named it twice, but New York has inspired composers to pen far more than its share of charismatic songs of romance and nostalgia. These tunes are still hummed, whistled and sung in karaoke bars around the world through old and young lips alike, and you can call for a Manhattan cocktail in most city bars across this planet and receive one without a frown or glimmer of hesitation.

Don't get me wrong, I love my hometown of London. It has a long, strong and fascinating history, but it doesn't have what New York, New York has in spades – glamour, romance and pizzazz. Just the mention of the name creates a frisson of expectation.

Despite a notorious and muddy history – the brooding presence of organised crime syndicates; racial disharmony; widespread drug abuse; extortion; one of the highest crime rates in the world – this entertainment and financial nerve centre has managed to fan a reputation of near fairytale proportions, dating back to long before Mr Francis Albert Sinatra crooned his way into our perceptions of this cramped little island.

The thought entered my brain: would this intoxicating mix of glamour and danger still be present?

That meeting – that unexpected skin-tingling offer – was still playing in my head as our British Airways plane landed with two bumps and an audible skid at JFK International Airport at 9.05 p.m. local time. When we finally plodded out of the airport we slid into one of the endless lines of waiting cabs. I told the taxi driver to take us to the Holiday Inn on West 57th between 8th and 9th Avenues – I think it sounds really cool to say those New York addresses.

I don't know why this location should impress me so, because no imagination whatsoever has been employed in the layout of Manhattan. It is just a grid and, of the very few street names, none could be described as exotic, but this city possessed a simplistic power that intrigued me.

I was disappointed to get a Pakistani cab driver who couldn't speak a word of English (or American). I have nothing against Pakistanis but I wanted a pucker New York cab driver such as the ones you see in the movies. I wanted to listen to his New York drawl and talk to him about his life and experiences in America's most talked about metropolis.

His like, along with architecture and customs are the very taste of a city. It would be the same if I had travelled to Pakistan – the last thing I would want is an American taxi driver picking me up. A location loses its identity and a certain amount of authenticity, somehow, when its indigenous race no longer work in important jobs like driving a taxi.

They, as well as shopkeepers and restaurant staff, are the public face of a country. I am well aware that nearly every city and major town in the world has a growing cosmopolitan element, but I still think it's a shame when a wonderful place like New York loses its fundamental character through excessive cultural diversity. There, I've said it.

As we approached Brooklyn Bridge my first impression was one of awe. It was the first steel-wire suspension bridge to be built, all six thousand feet of it, and was lit up like a Christmas tree. Lines of glittering bulbs, like electrically-charged strings of pearls, were looped theatrically between the two robust, arched limestone towers, showcasing this impressive viaduct in a way that made my skin tingle. It was akin to being welcomed on to a dramatically lit stage. I turned to Deb. 'This prime piece of artistry puts Putney Bridge in the Conference League,' I said, using a football analogy.

'First of all,' Deb replied, whilst looking out onto this shimmering New York City welcome mat, 'there are too many 'p's in that sentence and, secondly, I don't have a clue what the Conference League is.'

Connecting Brooklyn to Manhattan, the bridge was designed by John Augustus Roebling. It cost 15.5 million dollars and twenty-seven people died during its construction. On the day it opened, 24th May 1883, some poor sod had the unenviable job of counting the amount of traffic that trundled over it. The results of his mind-numbing labours revealed that one thousand eight hundred vehicles and one hundred and fifty thousand people crossed the East River that day. It carried elevated trains until 1944 and streetcars, the equivalent of our trams, until 1950.

On 30th May, six days after it opened, some unspeakable twat spread a rumour that the construction was about to collapse, causing a stampede in which twelve people were crushed to death. As far as I know, the imbecile was never identified.

P.T. Barnum, recognising a great opportunity to publicise his circus, helped squash the rumours concerning its stability, when his most famous attraction, Jumbo the elephant, led twenty-one of his hefty, trunk-swinging mates over the bridge. Great stunt, but I have a bit of sympathy for the bloke who was given a small dustpan and brush and told to clear up after the procession.

Ironically, the German born J.A. Roebling's involvement in the planning of its magnificent design was to be the death of him. During a survey at the East River site the designer's right foot was pinned against a pylon and crushed by a docking ferry. He had to have his toes amputated and shortly after that he developed tetanus. As the infection worsened he went on to suffer severe seizures, lapsed into a coma and died in the early hours of 22nd June 1869. Not the most glorious end to a talented man's life and probably not the way he would have wanted to go. His thirty-two-year-old son, Washington

Roebling, was placed in charge of the project and, despite his own ill-health, saw it through to its completion.

I had visited these shores twenty-five years ago and remember hardly anything from that time; certainly not this wonderful piece of architecture. It was a short business trip and all four days were spent with clients in downtown bars in an alcohol fuelled daze. Even so, I am amazed that a stirring sight, such as the Brooklyn Bridge, could have faded to a washed-out sepia in my memory?

'Wow, look at that!' said Deb. 'I've only ever approached New York in the hours of daylight. This is something else.' And it was. Peering through the strands of illuminated steel we were treated to another breathtaking sight. The night sky over Manhattan was pushed high by massive, shimmering, multi-windowed buildings that punctured the darkness above. From a distance the city appeared to be beneath a luminous dome. The encompassing spectrum of light started with a splash of fluorescent lemon yellow at its base, watery orange merged into pale violet, bleeding into crimson and indigo that melted into midnight blue, finally disappearing into black. It was a stunning introduction to New York City.

The buildings were like incandescent soldiers placed so close together there appeared to be no space between them whatsoever. The majesty of these monoliths was no better portrayed than by the MetLife Building. It stood like a colossal, square-shouldered concierge, positioned smack in the middle of Park Avenue. At night it was dramatically lit and appeared to be guarding Grand Central Station which sat at its feet.

It was now close to eleven p.m. As we proceeded through the trellis of city streets towards our temporary lodgings, I was mesmerised by the steam rising up into the cold night air from the road drains and raised flues. It put me in mind of so many wonderful movies I had watched as a youngster. Everywhere I looked there were shadowy Irish bars, brightly-lit bustling restaurants and tall, tall buildings.

New York had just experienced its worst weather for decades and was still in the grip of an uncompromising winter. Uneven piles of waxen snow with dirt-soaked, grey-brown edges lined the street gutters. Roofs, the ones that were low enough to be visible, were still snow covered; shop awnings glistened, fringed with spikes of icicles.

Dark, blurry figures, which looked as if they had walked straight out of an L.S. Lowry painting, moved diagonally and with purpose, sparring with the biting wind. I rejoiced in the charm of this moving picture displayed through the window of our canary-yellow taxi.

When we arrived at our hotel, I helped the bellboy take our luggage from the boot and load it on to a trolley. I paid the driver and tipped him five dollars. He said nothing – didn't even blink – then drove off into the night.

The hotel was OK. It was a Holiday Inn so I knew what to expect. It was warm, clean and unspectacular. After handing over passports and signing lengthy forms stating that we were not asylum seekers, the bellboy showed us to our room on the eighth floor. He took our suitcases from the baggage trolley and deposited them just inside the hallway. I followed him in with my golf clubs and guitar.

He waited. Despite having done half of his work I generously, or so I thought, tipped him three dollars. He looked positively underwhelmed. 'I suppose a *have a nice day* is out of the question!' I called after him as he sloped silently off in the direction of the lift (sorry, elevator).

I looked at Deb in astonishment. 'Bugger me, Deb! I've been in this country for just a few hours and I hand out two, by no means measly, gratuities and get a response similar to if I'd given them a slap across the face and pissed in their shoes. I wish I had have done now.'

Deb was now lying on her pencil-wide bed giggling. 'It has been a long day and you're tired and grumpy!'

'Yes I am. I'm tired and grumpy 'cos I've just paid eight bloody dollars to feel like a skinflint.'

'You'll feel better tomorrow after a good night's sleep.'

'Mmm! How much tip, do you suggest, I leave for that?'

Although I felt a bit weary, I was still buzzing from the sights of New York and was certainly not in the mood to sleep. Thankfully, neither was Deb, so we scooted down to the hotel bar for some refreshment. Disappointingly, the bar had the décor and ambience of a dentist's waiting room and the barmaid was worse. She stood, talking to another hotel employee, filing her nails for what seemed like hours, until I started to smash a few mirrors behind the bar to get her attention.

So, after a quick bottle of beer each, the cost of which was approximately half of my U.K. annual Council Tax bill we walked down to DJ's, an Irish bar on the corner of 55th and 8th.

Ah! They sell draught Bass. 'Pint of Bass and a glass of dry white wine please.'

The barman, who was the owner, was called PJ. This was a bit confusing as we were sitting in his bar named DJ's. But he was Irish and very drunk, so who was I to argue? Halfway through my pint, which tasted nothing like the Bass in my local, I discovered a very large and ugly insect, of a variety I'd never seen before, crawling up the inside of my glass.

PJ noticed the creature as well, plucked it from the receptacle, walked to the door and threw it outside.

'Sorry bout that. I fokken' barred him last night. I can't believe he's shown his face in here again!' Laughs all round from the small gathering of drinkers at the bar. He then poured my beer in to a fresh glass. 'Der you are. He won't have pissed in dat one.' More laughter.

The fact that it was the same beer didn't seem to register in his whisky filled brain, but it's impossible not to warm to the Irish sense of humour so I smiled, dipped my head and drank. We went on to spend another enjoyable hour in his company before Deb and I retired back to our small hotel room. Now, totally done in we stumbled over our unpacked luggage (the hotel was only booked for two nights) and into two skinny single beds that the Holiday Inn had provided for our comfort. The priority tomorrow was to find a suitable apartment for the rest of our stay.

But why, you may ask, had we taken flight over a pinch of England followed by an amplitude of Atlantic Ocean to arrive at New York in the first place? Perhaps now would be a good time to tell you a little about me and why my wife and I found ourselves in this pint-sized Manhattan bolt-hole.

Chapter Two

I was eight years old when I first experienced the wonder of travel. My parents took me and my older brother to the Isle of Sheppey which, roughly translated, is the isle of sheep. It was full of them. Everywhere you looked; sheep. They masticated, in their thousands, across endless acres of boggy marshland; baa'd aimlessly beside every stretch of cobbled road and dusty track; clip-clopped their cloven-hoofed way through each town, village and hamlet and were the plat du jour on every pub and restaurant menu throughout the entire island. This place was not short of sheep shit, I can tell you.

But I loved it. I revelled in being somewhere else, for the first time in my short life, other than our council flat in Wimbledon; especially as our two-bedroom home wasn't beside the seaside and nowhere near sheep. I remember crouching for hours, my sandals balanced precariously on seaweed-covered rocks, which had trapped captivating pools of water during the North Sea's temporary beach evacuation. I'd be searching for crabs and any signs of marine life.

The Isle of Sheppey lies just off the northern coast of Kent and although not the longest hike from Wimbledon, at eight years of age it seemed like another world. We stayed just outside the town of Sheerness and all I can remember of the place was the lovely lack of concrete, the unfamiliar, exotic smell of the sea and the novelty of having to use an outside toilet.

The wooden structure was placed at the end of a long, slim garden. (Why on earth would you erect something on your property as vitally important as a privy at the furthest point away from your living quarters?) It was cold and draughty and the door didn't shut properly. If you were doing a sit down job it was an outstretched foot and hope for the best. But to a little boy, spoilt by an in-house council flat loo, it was an adventure. It wasn't a lavatory; it was a place to hide, a spaceship, a private escape from the grown-ups. I can't recollect looking forward so much to having a pee or a poo before that wonderful holiday – or since, now I think of it.

And there it was. The simple wonder of travel.

As the years sailed blithely past and deep into my sketchy memory it was always the holidays that remained undamaged by the erosion of time. And, of course, when blessed with the power of earning my own money my choice of destination became more ambitious. The Isle of Wight was briskly followed by France, Portugal and, well, you get the picture.

Those early passing years that appeared to drift and tack in the wind, much to my horror, kept gathering pace, soon to resemble the stones we used to skim across the froth of the incessant waves. My life, it seemed, had shot off in a mad dash and left me behind. And twenty-five years of working in the City as a foreign exchange broker was more than enough for any semi-sane individual. I needed to make a decision.

I decided to become a writer.

One year later, I sat at my computer, alone, words trickling from my fingertips. I say alone; I was accompanied by a cup of coffee, two Hobnobs and a pile of rejection letters that could have filled Santa's sack. I was in contemplative mood. Was this a good idea? Moreover, I was beginning to receive looks of embarrassment on informing my friends that I was now an unpublished author. In the painfully short time it takes to ruin a hard-earned reputation, I'd gone from being Billy-big-dick to, well, dick.

My wife, Deborah, still worked in the City selling financial analysis to bank traders and had just returned from a four-day business trip to her New York office. After I had made her a cup of much-missed tea she gave me a brief summary of her visit. The overriding message was that the office was struggling and in need of motivation. I suggested, in a casual manner, that she should apply for a three-month secondment to the lack-lustre office with me, naturally, being part of the package. During that period she could sort out their problems and enhance her career at the same time.

Little did I expect, two months later, to be the surprised recipient of an all expenses paid invitation to up sticks and hang out in Manhattan for exactly three months. Blimey! That was easy. I made a note to put forward more ambitious, *casual* suggestions in the future. I wondered if they had an office in the Maldives?

It was perfect timing. For the first time in my life, I was in the fortunate position of having no job to tie me down to the country of my birth. If my writing career was going nowhere, there was no logical reason why I should have to follow it.

But three months in Manhattan – what new delights; what fresh challenges; what the hell was I going to do with *my* time?

Whilst Deb's task was to gee up an inert sales team I thought my mission, if I decided to accept it, should be to discover whether New York, New York was, in fact, the iconic city lauded in countless nostalgic songs, effusive books, jolly musicals and crime-filled movies. Could Manhattan live up to a reputation that may just have outgrown itself over the years of media obsession? Just as importantly, could I live with the reputed, frenzied pace of life on what was going to be, for me at least, an extended three month vacation?

I remember once being told never to wash my or anyone else's dirty linen in public. I asked myself whether this piece of advice should apply to a city big enough to look after itself. A decision was made. My goal would be to observe and scribble – to show it all – report the smiles, the frowns, the ups and downs of Manhattan's public and not so public face. And tucked in the mix during those thirteen weeks would be my experiences and musings, whilst being a minute particle of this mad little island.

So, on a drowsy dawn Friday morning, which was both wintry cold and the 20th February 2004, we prepared ourselves to say farewell to everything familiar. We had spent the previous two days packing our entire life into four suitcases. A legion of corpulent luggage, zipped and padlocked, guitar and golf clubs were slid down the stairs to the front door.

We were off to New York for three months. How exciting! How bloody scary! Would my house still be there on my return? More worryingly, would England still be there? I felt slightly uneasy, almost vulnerable, leaving my snug English womb for a loose-fitting Yankee surrogate.

My next door neighbour John, a retired policeman, had kindly agreed to take Deborah and me to the airport. He is a very friendly chap, very generous in body and nature and owns a people carrier – perfect. He is also a slave to routine. He only ever wears grey polyester trousers and his old police-issue off-white shirts, open at the collar and sleeves rolled to the elbow. It can be arctic Alaska or sizzling Serengeti, it makes no difference to him.

The knock on my door infused me with a rush of adrenalin. The time had arrived. I opened the door and a blast of freezing cold February air pushed rudely past me. 'Hi, John, almost there – I think.' John was wearing grey polyester trousers and an off-white, open-necked shirt with sleeves rolled to the elbow. He smiled knowingly and ambled back to sit in his people carrier.

Five minutes later, after a final house-check, John and I managed to get our mountain of baggage into his car. He had kindly taken most of the back seats out to accommodate it all.

As I locked the front door I stepped back and admired my house, as though I had just finished building it. I suddenly felt surprisingly reckless leaving our warm, detached haven that Deb and I moved into just under two years ago.

Pull yourself together Sullivan, you big girl's blouse, we're off to the Big Apple. 'Goodbye, Surrey home. Be good,' I said to the carefully arranged pile of bricks.

John pulled out of the driveway and just missed a passing Fiat Uno. We screeched to a halt. Now wearing our luggage on our backs and our noses pressed up against the windscreen, John spoke for the first time that morning:

'Sorry 'bout that. Blimey! That was almost a good start to your trip.'

As I released three bruised knuckles from his ashtray and watched them turn from white to bluey-pink, I wondered if this was an omen.

We arrived at Heathrow alive and in good time and made it to the front of the passenger queue, which zigzagged through a confusing maze of tape-lined barriers, passed all our worldly goods to the British Airways check-in girl and managed to negotiate front of aisle seats with bags of leg room. Result! The flight was a bit bumpy and the service was smooth, but we'd arrived.

So there it was: why we were here and sleeping one hundred feet above the beeline sidewalks and perennial traffic of USA's financial district.

Chapter Three

I woke at eight a.m. Rising from my bed, jet-lagged and feeling like I hadn't slept a wink, I tripped over our baggage once again, raked my shinbone down the protruding padlock and said, 'Fuck it!' – which didn't help one bit.

My wife, who's a much better sleeper than I am (which is the only thing I don't like about her) did not stir despite my hopping around and audible cursing. Ignoring the fact that I was in urgent need of medical attention I carried on through to the bathroom for a morning wee to discover the bath had been custom made for *Bashful*. Danny DeVito would have struggled to bathe in this piddly piece of porcelain.

Too tired to descend eight floors and search for the dining room we had breakfast in our room – two greasy fried eggs, bacon that had been gently griddled for three days and something called "skillets". They looked remarkably similar to hamster droppings but, hot-diggity-dog, they turned out to be the highlight on the plate.

As I was going to be unemployed for the duration of our stay, Deb had managed to procure a laptop from her company. With this miraculous piece of technology I could write my journal and keep in touch with the rest of the world through the wonders of web and email. Trouble was, it appeared to be powered by steam. Searching for an apartment on the internet was achingly slow; tying messages around the legs of pigeons would have been quicker.

I tried all morning to find something clean and acceptable for us in which to spend our next thirteen weeks, but without any luck. The process was worse than useless. When I did hit upon a satisfactory apartment it was either too dear, too small or I couldn't contact the realtor. I resorted to using the payphone in our room but after being put through to numerous wrong extensions I gave up.

I then discovered our hotel had two public PC's in the lobby downstairs, so Deb and I tried our luck on them. Unfortunately, we still appeared to be going round and round in circles and getting nowhere fast. Added to that, I had to keep stuffing ten-dollar bills in to its greedy mouth, every other minute, to access websites that wanted to sign me up for life insurance or sell me anything from haemorrhoid preparations to nose-hair trimmers before giving me my required information.

Can't computers be the most annoying fucking things you've ever come across in your lifetime? It was occasions such as this that caused me to reassess my opinion of traffic wardens.

Do you remember the days when you could pick up a telephone, insert your index finger into a series of small holes in a shiny metal wheel, flick it back and forth a few times and speak to a human being? Wonderful, wasn't it?

I just thought of a great way to make my fortune – buy a lorry-load of PC's and rent them out to hotels.

Just at that point, the waitress behind the nearby patronless bar put a CD of rap music on at disco volume level.

I glanced over at Deb, who appeared to be conducting a similarly fruitless search on the neighbouring computer. Her face reflected my mood.

'How's it going over there?' I asked, lifting my voice above the cacophonous barrage.

'Pardon?' she replied. 'Oh, this is hopeless. That's it! The last thing I need is bad attitude music to go with my bad attitude that is getting worse by the minute. I hate rap music.' She got up from her computer.

'Mmm! I'm with you. I never thought I'd hear myself say this, but Des O'Connor singing Dick-A-Dum-Dum would be a much welcomed change right now,' I replied.

Let's face it, rap is not the most melodic music... or friendly. Watching it being performed is even worse; what's all that with the pointy fingers?

I stood, stretched and breathed deep. 'Had enough?' I asked.

Deb managed a weary nod.

We decided to vacate the hotel before doing something drastic, like, leave the country, so we took a walk through Central Park, some ten minutes stroll away. This was better. It was three p.m. and the sun was shining. The park was much bigger than I realised and contained an unusual amount of very old people; lean, serious and ridiculous-looking cyclists all kitted out with kaleidoscopic skintight lycras and us.

This was before lycra, in any significant volume, had reached our shores. The only cyclists that I recall making regular use of our roads, up to this point in my lifetime, were old postmen with shiny-peaked flat caps and the occasional village policeman; both of which wore moustaches and steel bicycle clips. These clips were clamped around ankles to stop flapping trousers getting caught in whirling chains thus throwing the merry, carefree rider headlong over the handlebars.

So, whatever happened to bicycle clips? In fact, whatever happened to moustaches? In the first three quarters of the last century, moustaches were found lingering beneath an impressively high percentage of male noses – and the odd female one. My Aunt Nellie sported a particularly splendid growth that bristled just above her red lipstick, which meant kissing her goodbye was to be avoided if at all possible.

In fact, in 1916 British soldiers were required by regulation to wear a tash as a sign of military esprit. But for some reason, I've yet to discover, they've virtually disappeared from the face of, if not the earth, then the male population of Great Britain.

Anyway, back to New York. The evidence of the city's worst winter for more than twenty years was far more apparent in the park. Most of the grass was covered in glistening sheets of snow and every fifty yards or so there were huge piles of the stuff where the paths had been cleared. Despite being swathed in jumpers, coats and scarves the bitter wind began to scythe through the layers of our clothes.

As we reached one of the many park exits we were relieved to see the very impressive looking Plaza Hotel with restaurant and BAR in front of us. It sat on the corner of Central Park South and 5th Avenue and was truly a majestic structure. It was built in 1907, when most of the suites were occupied as permanent residences, and designed by Henry Janeway Hardenbergh in the style of a French Renaissance

Chateau. Henry, despite having a bit of a girly middle name, was quite a clever little chap and clearly an industrious one, as his services were much sought after. Amongst countless others, he tendered his creative skills to the design of the original Waldorf Hotel and the imposing Dakota luxury apartment building, where the great John Lennon used to reside.

The Plaza proved to be a wonderful place in which to warm ourselves. As we wandered around the calming innards it was as if we were stepping back in time to days of great wealth and old-fashioned values – a pleasant surprise in progressive New York.

The interior was adorned with carved bronze fittings, luxurious carpets and gilded ceilings that towered above satiny marble walls. Quiet rooms and corridors were adorned with strategically placed lush floral displays exuding a stylish calm. The Oak Room restaurant and separate Oak Bar both had wood panelling as dark as plain chocolate, with Everett Shinn murals adorning the walls. Shinn (1876-1953) was an artist, playwright and actor – a talented and busy man by the sound of it. But for me, his most illustrious achievement, a largely unknown fact, was to design the famous "Shinn pad", used to protect the lower legs of British soccer players. They are still used to this very day. Good work, Ev.

After a relaxed browse amid all this splendour we then had to wait in a small queue, would you believe, before the immaculately attired, eight-foot-two-inch, saturnine doorman allowed us in to the Oak Bar, purely for a drink. Despite having to ring my bank manager to arrange a loan for two rounds of liquid refreshment it was worth it. I was in New York's finest surrounded by affluence and nourished by beer – I could think of worse scenarios. Even the complimentary mixed nuts that filled the cut glass bowl on our lovingly burnished oak table were worth writing home about.

As Tony Oettinger once said, "Time flies like an arrow; fruit flies like a banana." And just to prove this, darkness had fluttered downwards outside our place of leisure in a blink. The city was now getting ready for the evening's revellers and we wanted our two limey faces to be amongst them. So, we returned to our hotel to get spruced up.

After having showered in our sink we ventured out to Kennedy's for a few pre-meal drinks – there were less Irish bars in Dublin than this place. The atmosphere, along with the taped music, was very lively and each Irish barman had a story to tell.

Why is it that the Irish are so full of stories? The school curriculum in Ireland must do nothing but teach storytelling!

'And how many GCSE's have you got, Paddy?

'Five.'

'And what might they be?'

'Basic Storytelling, Advanced Storytelling, Amusing Yarns, Tall Tales and Complete Fokken Lies.'

The Guinness was a welcome treat from the fizzy American beer but had not sailed across the Atlantic with complete success. I am not saying it wasn't quaffable though. Glasses emptied, we wandered across one block to the corner of 57th and 7th where a proud, dusty-pink-bricked Carnegie Hall was waiting to greet us. This again was a building that raised my adrenalin levels a few nicks. Andrew Carnegie awarded the commission to William Burnet Tuthill who completed the construction in 1891.

Here's an interesting fact: dear old Andy must have been a trusting soul because Tuthill had never before designed a concert hall, but he conceived not only an elegant building but one with spectacular acoustics. Strangely, it was the first and last one he ever built. I suppose if you achieve perfection at your first attempt why risk buggering up your reputation with further efforts.

Not only the finest orchestras in the world but greats such as Billie Holiday, Duke Ellington, Shirley Bassey and, one of my heroes, Groucho Marx, amongst others too numerous to mention, have all entertained to packed houses at the revered venue. It contained three halls. The main hall, the Isaac Stern Auditorium, could seat over two thousand eight hundred bottoms. The other two presented jazz events, lectures and forums.

Whilst we stood gawping at the impressive structure we realised that we were standing with our backs to the Trattoria dell'Arte.

'Hungry?' I asked Deb.

'Mmm,' was enough of an answer for me.

It was a modest looking, basically furnished diner which sat on the opposite corner to the Hall. As we entered, an over-friendly waiter approached us with a smile that made Jack Nicholson's portrayal of The Joker appear self-conscious.

'My name's Aubrey. How can I help you two lovely people this evening?'

Well! What incredible intuition this man possessed. We just had to stay. He joyfully acceded to my wish of a cosy window table, scattering rose petals at our feet along the way. From here we could people-watch as they entered the famous concert hall.

I was still feeling quite thirsty and asked the waiter, who was by now my best friend, if they sold Guinness.

'No, sir. Why don't you try a Brooklyn Brown? It tastes like Newcastle Brown – if you've ever tried that?'

Have I ever tried Newky Brown? Was George Michael partial to a public toilet?

The beer, amazingly, tasted just like Newcastle Brown and despite it being served up in a flower vase I was impressed. The waiter was so happy for me I was expecting him to leave me something in his will, or at least ask me to dance. As it turned out, he did neither. We went on to have an agreeable meal and were enjoying the chatty ambience of the place until the bill arrived. They, of course, call it the check. Surely, a cheque is what you pay the bill with? And just to confuse the issue even more, what do they call their dollars? Bills!

Anyway, whatever you called the damn thing, it had the unfriendly amount of one hundred and forty-five dollars (about eighty pounds) slapped on the bottom of it – this was 2004, remember. That was for two modest main courses, two small glasses of wine and a bloody Brooklyn Brown. And there was me thinking that Elliot Ness along with his Untouchables had got extortion under control.

In a state of shock with this display of undisguised greed, I left a niggardly ten-dollar tip. As we got up to leave, our waiter, who would have gladly let me use his head as a footstool throughout my meal, suddenly turned into a woman scorned. I have never seen a look of such hostility and utter loathing on a man's face before or since. At one point I thought he was going to scream RAPE!

As we reached the door on our way out, I turned. 'Same time, next week, Aub,' I called with a wink and a wave, as veins began bursting from his temples.

Obviously, his previous boot-licking performance was just to receive an obscene tip to go with the obscene price of the meal. This man should be an actor. (Maybe he was).

It didn't take me long to suss out the mentality of American waiters.

~~

Our small room looked out onto the inner well of our hotel, which was not wonderfully inspiring. But the square foot of sky, visible by pressing my cheek against the window and crushing vertebra four in to vertebra five of my neck, was clear blue. A golden shaft of sunshine speared down into the bottom of the well, lighting up the hotel kitchen's gargantuan rubbish bins – or, rather, garbage bins – which gave me hope for the day ahead. That was until Deb presented me with a cup of weak tea made in our room coffee percolator (we had no teapot) and served in a Styrofoam cup. I can't even begin to describe the taste to you.

'Right! Today, we are not going to eat the awful hotel breakfast,' Deb announced, seeing my reaction to the stomach churning beverage. 'I'm treating you to something special.' My tall, slim, blonde wife, all at once, appeared even more attractive as my eyes ignited and sent my imagination running around in circles chasing its own tail.

As Deb had been here on recent short business trips she had a better knowledge of the city than me. So, today she decided we were going to take an early morning marathon walk downtown to visit the meatpacking district – their equivalent, I suppose, of our Smithfield Market. Unfortunately, being Sunday, it was closed but the area was, supposedly, still full of character even in its deserted state.

The trip, though, was not to buy meat or even watch it being packed but to get a general feel of the city and take breakfast in Pastis. This was for two reasons. The hotel breakfast was close to being condemned and the chic restaurant, frequented by the rich and famous was renowned for providing the most scrumptious breakfasts in the civilised world.

After a good hour's interesting walk in sunshine and freezing wind we reached our destination – or did we? The area was like a ghost town and I refused to believe that such a revered eatery could exist and thrive in the middle of nowhere. Surely, Deb had got it wrong? It was just before nine a.m. and we were the only people, it seemed, on the planet. I was now weary, my feet and back were aching and I was prepared to eat any scraps of food from the floor that the meat traders may have dropped from Saturday's market.

'I'm sure it's somewhere around here!' Deb said, beginning to lose faith in herself.

'Well if it's not, at least there's no-one around to witness me killing you with my bare hands.'

'I'm sure this is the place. Mind you, it was a year ago that I was taken here and it was by taxi.'

'Have I told you lately that I love you?' I asked.

'No!' she replied, hopefully.

'Good!'

As we turned yet another deserted corner, like an oasis, it appeared. It was a modest, faded brick building with a red canopy announcing its name. Outside was a number of metal and plastic raffia-type chairs scattered around a few silver pedestal tables. It was ten below and blowing a gale. Who were these tables for... penguins?

My relief at finding the place was immediately tempered by the sight of eight people waiting in a queue outside the front door. They were all, without exception, various shades of blue. 'This joint must be the dog's bollocks if there are people prepared to freeze to death to get in!' I whispered gently to Deb, as we took our place at the end of the line. There was no way, after a bracing three mile zig-zag across town that I was going to give up now, so we waited.

It was worth it. Twenty minutes later the doors opened to us and we were ushered into a French bistro affair that dripped with character. Heavy, faux-ancient cracked-white tiles covered the walls and floor, similar to that of Sweetings in London. The high ceilings dropped large, globular glass lights from slim brass arms, like enormous lollipops above our heads. The table tops and crescent-shaped bar were made of a veiny off-white marble with a matt finish that you couldn't see your face in. And the place was buzzing: it was filled with bohemian musician types, well-heeled aristos, gregarious actor sorts, outrageous posers, and me and Deb.

I had the poached eggs and mushrooms in thick, dark gravy and it was delicious. Deb had the lusty cheese encrusted onion soup (I never knew that soup could be lusty – must get out more) which also received top marks. Still hungry after our morning's arctic exertions we shared a Croque Madame, which roughly translated is a Mrs Crunchy.

It is a hot ham and cheese toasted sandwich with a poached egg on top – it was to die for. The Croque Monsieur is the same without the egg. As the French, bless 'em, have apparently associated the Croque Madame's "egg" with a woman's ovaries, you would have thought they could've stuck a sausage on the Croque Monsieur.

The brunch was expensive but we knew it would be. We both thoroughly enjoyed the hour and a half, watching all the characters watching each other. Alas, there were no well-known celebs. Then, in a polite but persuasive manner, we got kicked out to allow another two hypothermic victims to donate a fist full of dollars to the Help Mr Pastis Get Rich Quick Fund. Good fun but I am definitely in the wrong business.

Now warm and replete we walked back uptown to the tall and pointy Empire State Building. On its completion in 1931 it was the world's tallest building. That was to last for forty years until the North Tower of the World Trade Center was built. It was designed from the top downwards by Gregory Johnson which strikes me as a rather venturesome thing to do.

'Right. I've got this bloody great enormous long spike,' I can imagine him announcing to a startled entourage of builders and planners, 'now I need something fairly substantial to hold the bugger up. Any ideas?'

Building started on St Patrick's Day – 17th March 1930, involving three thousand four hundred workers, of which three died. The workforce comprised mostly of immigrants from various parts of Europe. Apparently, there was a bit of rivalry with 40 Wall Street and the Chrysler Building as to who could claim bragging rights for the tallest structure. Boys will be boys and size matters apparently. As we all know now, Greg turned out to have the biggest one.

Travelling to its summit was a "had to do whilst in New York" so we queued for thirty minutes, paid eleven dollars each and took the lift to the eightieth floor. I noted that the elevator took less time to reach eighty floors than our old council flat lift took to cover five and it didn't stink of stale urine either.

When we stopped I was amazed the lift was not full of nosebleeds and knickers around ankles. For some strange reason we then had to take another lift the remaining six floors to reach the top. Maybe elevators can only travel up eighty floors before getting mechanical vertigo?

Seeing another long line of people waiting for this relatively short trip to the summit we decided to take the stairs. Unfortunately, when attempting anything physical my mind is still stuck in the 1970s when I was lithe, fit and reckless. After the first two floors the muscles just above my knees began to tighten a touch. By the time we reached the fourth they refused, point blank, to cooperate at all and immediately turned to wood.

The trouble was, there was a wedge of jabbering Japanese tourists directly behind us. So, there was no way I was going to stop and lose face to these individuals. So, with gritted everything, I kept on climbing. With each step my lower limbs got stiffer and stiffer and my smile more fixed. As we started to climb the sixth flight, lower-body rigor mortis had set in and by the time we got to the top I was walking like Pinnochio.

This was confirmed by the high-pitched giggling that was coming from behind me.

I'm relieved to tell you the pain and humiliation was all worth it. As we walked out into the fresh air we were slapped across the face with stunning views across Manhattan. Flanked by the winding East River and Hudson River, New York became a collage of imperious buildings and multi-coloured roof tops, all proudly displaying their different shapes and sizes.

Thankfully, it was a clear day giving both clarity and perspective to our vista with the sun's platinum reflections dancing across both powerful looking rivers. We had a three-hundred-and-sixty degree panorama and could see for miles in every direction. The trouble was the wind was fierce and icy-cold, so ten minutes was all we could tolerate before we joined the queue to come down again.

The place was absolutely packed to the gunnels and at eleven dollars-a-go they must have been making a fortune – and that's without all the crappy paraphernalia that they were selling inside the building. I've just had another foolproof idea on how to make a fortune: build a bloody great building in the middle of a major city with a viewing platform on the top, whack in a few very fast lifts and charge people to go up and down in them all day. Since writing this, some so-and-so has pinched my idea: London now has the Shard.

Here are a few facts about the Empire State Building that will make you nudge your granny and whistle through your teeth. At 9.40 a.m. on Saturday 28th July 1945, a B-25 Mitchell bomber, piloted in thick fog by Lieutenant Colonel William Smith, crashed into the north side of the Empire State Building between the 79th and 80th floors. One of the plane's engines shot straight through the structure and landed on the roof of the adjoining building, starting a fire that destroyed a particularly splendid penthouse. The other engine and part of the landing gear plummeted down an elevator shaft. As a result of this disaster fourteen people lost their lives.

Now how's this for "Do you want the good news or the bad news"?

Elevator operator, Betty Lou Oliver, was badly burned by the impact but was successfully rescued. The rescuers then decided to lower her down in the elevator, not realising that the cables had been badly weakened in the accident. As they placed her inside, the cables snapped sending poor Betty Lou hurtling down past seventy-five floors to the basement – a damn sight faster than she or they had anticipated – where she had to be rescued once more. 'Thanks a lot, boys!' I hear her whimpering. The amazing thing is, she actually survived and was taken to hospital, mishap free, to be treated for her multiple injuries as well as her burns.

Despite the damage, the building was open the following Monday. Betty Lou, bless her, returned to work five months later, where her inspector complimented this amazing woman for her mental strength on being able to get back on the horse, as it were, and continue in the same job. I have to agree with him.

Her horrific plunge still stands today as a Guinness World Record for the longest survived elevator fall. Many people since have tried their damndest to break the record and failed, with obvious dire consequences.

I was also amazed to discover that more than thirty troubled souls have committed suicide from the top of the building. The fence that is in place today was erected in 1947 after five people, in a three-week span and presumably pissed-off with their lot, tried to jump to their deaths.

But this is the story that unhinged my jaw. In 1979, Elvita Adams jumped from the eighty-sixth floor hoping to end it all when a timely gust of wind blew her back to safety onto the floor below. So, instead of being scraped off the tarmac like a dollop of strawberry jam, she suffered only a broken hip and was told, in no uncertain terms, not to do it again. The question is: was she grateful that Mother Nature saved her miserable life or was she hopping mad that she failed to become part of the sidewalk? We'll never know.

Having released ourselves in a safe and generally accepted manner from the lofty place of astonishing stories, we walked back through Times Square which was full of colour and animation even by day. I couldn't wait to see it by night. Actually, there was one small negative to our brief visit there: Deb and I were almost killed three times crossing the road in the space of a few minutes whilst being seduced by our surroundings and looking the wrong way. So, I've renamed it Three Times Square.

My job is to find an apartment tomorrow. With wall-to-wall luggage carpeting the floor the hotel room was becoming increasingly claustrophobic. I was beginning to develop a strong sympathetic leaning towards the plight of sardines.

Chapter Four

'Right, I'm off. Wish me luck,' said my smart-suited wife.

I followed her to the hotel room door and gave her a kiss that said you don't need luck. 'Good luck,' I said, just in case.

This Monday morning heralded Deb's first day at work. An eight a.m. start in New York is very different to that of London. At home she has to get up at six a.m. to catch the train at 7.10 a.m. to reach the City by eight. Here she gets up at seven a.m. and leaves at 7.50 a.m. for a ten minute walk to work. No commuting and an extra hour in bed had already put a smile on her lovely face. I kissed her goodbye and trusted America's financial centre to look after her.

Propped up against the wall on the hotel bed, I sat in my underpants, checking my mobile phone messages over a plate of skillets which, I've now discovered, is the only edible food the hotel serves. My mobile was sadly lacking in the response department. Not one reply had I received from the mountain of messages that I had left on realtors' answerphones over the weekend.

Incidentally, skillet is, confusingly, the American word for frying pan. Who knows, maybe this place has a whole menu of kitchen utensils of which I've never heard? Tomorrow, perhaps, I'll try a plate of sun-dried saucepan lids or dip in to a basket of battered bread knives.

Frustrated, I popped over the road to the local newsagent and bought the English Daily Mail. The Indian proprietor charged me two dollars. At the current exchange rate that's one pound and twenty pence. It's forty pence at home. When I questioned the price he just shrugged his shoulders as if I'd just asked him who won the three thirty at Sandown Park. I picked up a *free* local property paper, which did not ease the pain at all, and plodded back to my hotel. Thumbing through the freebie, I saw "rooms to rent in hospitality apartment building", whatever that may be. So, I walked down to 49th and Lexington to check it out.

Oh dear! This was not what I was searching for; the traffic was bumper to fender and, rather annoyingly, everyone was leaning on their car horn. I don't mean a one second fingertip toot on the central part of the steering wheel like we do in England. I mean forearm smashing the steering column and keeping the rigid limb locked on until it was needed to manoeuvre the car again. The noise was a brain-swelling assault on my being. As far as I could see, the simple cause of the traffic jam was too many vehicles with not enough space. But that's what they did in New York: choleric car owners, who didn't require any valid reason for their intolerance levels to spontaneously combust, abounded throughout the latticework of streets and avenues. Who or what breeds these mentalities?

The "hospitality building" was smack on the corner of the busy junction. It was grey, drab and weary looking. They were demanding six hundred dollars a week for a one bedroom wardrobe – it would have been a tight squeeze fitting my luggage into it let alone living in the place for three months. I left the area feeling like a pauper in a kingdom of overpriced condominiums – disconsolate and somewhat lost.

So, back to the hotel to make more calls to over-exuberant, slick salesmen who promised the moon and stars, merely to produce not very fresh air. Ah, but Julio sounded different. He was born in Buenos Aires and sounded rather charming. The manner in which he conducted himself was close to credible; he kept to his word by calling back ten minutes later with two viewings.

The first viewing was on 38th between Park Avenue and Maddison. The area was lovely, the apartment was clean and well decorated... ah! Same problem. On the printed particulars of the property it stated in bold letters, No Pets. It should have read Just Pets – it was tiny. Then, what can you expect for two thousand five hundred dollars a month? This area of real estate was patently way out of our price range.

The second was on 72nd and Columbus – that's Upper West and almost overlooking Central Park. Julio, (pronounced hhhoooleeeo) who used to be a tour guide, told me the Dakota Apartments were just around the corner and insisted on showing them to me. When we arrived, he pointed to the exact spot where one of my heroes of music, John Lennon, was mindlessly gunned down.

Quite unexpectedly, I got a sudden shiver that travelled the length of my spine. A mixture of melancholy and horror enveloped me as my imagination re-enacted the chilling scene. It was a depressing thought that a deranged American sad-sack could purchase a gun as easy as an Englishman could buy a toothbrush and shoot someone dead. Not that you can shoot someone dead with a toothbrush, but you know what I mean.

I was falling in love with New York but part of me will never forgive this city for harbouring and supplying the means to twisted fruitcakes who can simply eliminate the likes of J. Lennon Esquire. There was only one.

The apartment we viewed was in a classy and clearly expensive area but the rooms themselves were soulless. I was now developing a nagging sense of despondency rapidly supported by a nagging sense of thirst. My watch told me that five p.m. had just come and gone so, after Julio had departed, I gave Deb a quick ring and arranged to meet her outside the Dakota building.

After repeating the same depressing slaying of a Beatle story to her we went on walkabout around Upper West Manhattan. There appeared to be more Italian restaurants up this side and the pace of life was just a little slower. The Irish bars still abounded and we eventually found ourselves in "Malachi's". The owner was called Shaun.

I very often have trouble in these Irish bars... and it's always with the owners. They've all got such quirky personalities that the prospect of a swift drink turns into a session before you can say, 'Just a half for me, Shaun, me old friend, me old mucker – I must be off.'

As Deborah and I sat at the highly polished, mahogany-substitute bar discussing the finer points of real estate a sudden and unwelcome weight descended upon my right shoulder. My ear on the same side was then treated to a blast of hot, putrid air as a bubble of unsteady words began to emerge from the alcoholic wind tunnel.

'Hey, Paddy! D'ya have a fuckin' happy hour in this place?' It came from a bear of an American who wore a very loud, large-checked lumberjack shirt, paint-spattered jeans and the biggest pair of boots I have ever seen. In fact, they were bigger than half the apartments I had viewed that morning. He was also swaying dangerously close to my pint of Guinness.

'How did ya know me name was Paddy?' Shaun drilled back.

'Well, you're a fuckin' Irish leprechaun, aintcha? So, I just guessed.'

I smelled trouble. I tried to appear completely oblivious of the rude drunk and continued my conversation with Deb.

'You're obviously very good at guessing, mister,' Shaun replied. 'If you can guess what I'm going to say next, you can have happy hour drinks all night.'

The drunk, not very big on sarcasm, looked confused. 'Just give me a goddam beer.'

'No. Wrong answer, pal. I was going to say "Feck off outta me bar, you fat drunk, or I'll call the cops!" Bad luck, you lost.'

This was not what he wanted to hear. Or me, come to that. With a growl he picked up my unguarded pint of Guinness, which was at least half full, and drunk it down in one enormous gulp. Oh gawd! I really didn't want to get involved in all this aggravation but now I had no option.

'Oi! What the bloody hell you doin', mate? That's my drink and it's gonna cost you five dollars.' Even as the words were leaving my lips I couldn't believe I was talking to this hostile monster in such an aggressive manner. He made Popeye's adversary, Bluto, look like Wayne Sleep.

'You fuckin' Irish?' he slurred.

'No! I'm fucking English and you owe me a pint of fucking Guinness,' I replied, trying to sound hard. I held my breath as he moved his massive fist towards my unbroken, defenceless nose. I didn't move; I figured that if I didn't show him I was scared he might back off. Instead of spreading my hooter all over my face he unfurled his hand and a grubby ten dollar note fluttered down into my lap.

'You're OK, buddy. My grandmother was English.'

And with that, he patted me on the cheek and snaked out of the bar.

'And let that be a lesson to you!' I called after him, when I was confident he couldn't possibly hear me. 'We need somewhere to live,' I added, 'don't wanna sell me your boots do you?' Thank God I didn't tell him that many years ago my ancestors were Irish. He could have been in big trouble.

Because of the kerfuffle we, naturally, had to stay with the barman to give him moral support. We supported him, unselfishly, for two more rounds of drinks. Four pints of Guinness and four Bloody Mary's into our evening I slurred for the bill.

'That's twenty dollars, my man,' said Shaun.

It didn't take my jumbled brain very long to work out that it had cost me just twelve pounds in real money for me and Deb to lose the power of coherent speech. I think his unbounded generosity had a lot to do with his customer's dalliance with serious life-changing injuries.

Now on a high, we tripped gaily into Café D'arte. The word around town that we had endured a harrowing evening must have spread because the Filipino waiters greeted us like long-lost relatives. This manifested itself in the staff providing three copious courses of lovingly cooked vittles for the munificent price of thirty-five dollars.

How are you on coincidences? I've heard a few hard-to-believe ones in my time, but not many top this one. We were served by Maria, an American waitress aged about twenty. Very attractive and very pleasant, in a way that said "I'm not after a tip, I'm just a really nice person". On hearing our accents she asked us where we hailed from.

'I come from Essex,' said Deb.

'Oh my God! My mother was born in Essex,' said the waitress.

'Really! What part?' Deb replied, much surprised.

'A little place called Leigh-on-sea.'

'I was brought up in Leigh-on-sea, and so was my mother,' said Deb.

After much plummeting of the surrounding jaws the waitress insisted in running off to phone her mother, who now lived in New York, to tell her this amazing piece of news. Deb and I, thinking we'd never see her again, got stuck into our steaks.

Steaks? These expanses of flesh, so voluminous, gave credence to my belief that America had rediscovered, and was successfully breeding, the dinosaur. The "economy meal", which I took to mean the economy of a small principality, was served with a side bucket of french fries. A sprig of parsley and three button mushrooms had been squeezed onto each plate to demonstrate a touch of finesse.

After twenty minutes of voracious eating, with the plates appearing to be as full as when we started, the waitress reappeared. She asked if she could join us at the table. I was half-hoping she was going to produce a knife and fork to help me finish off my meal. The Tyrannosaurus Rexburger had now transformed itself, in my mind, from benign, tasty sustenance to the nutritional equivalent of a school bully.

'Yes, of course,' I said, 'pull up a chair.'

'Well you're never gonna believe this!' she began. It turned out that her mother, now living in New York, went to the same school as Deb's mother. They were in the same year and, although not friends, knew each other very well. At around the same time and unknown to either of them, they sailed to Canada as young women. Deb's mum met and married a Scotsman, gave birth to Deb then moved back to Essex. Maria's mum went on to marry a Canadian, had Maria, also moved back to Essex and then on to the States. Spooky eh?

It got me thinking. I wonder how many other amazing coincidences we are simply unaware of throughout our lives. Apparently, so I've read since, this occurrence is not as unusual as we may think. Statisticians will tell you that the odds of probability are a good deal higher than the rest of us mathematical dimwits imagine. Many a laudable brain over the years has attributed these incredible coincidences to such things as telepathy, ESP, premonitions – the list goes on. I'm not sure I go along with any of those theories but I am somewhat fascinated by these chance happenings.

Here's just three that got me thinking.

Desperate to find his long-lost daughter Lisa, carpenter Michael Dick travelled from Bow, East London, to Sudbury in Suffolk. The local paper, in support, ran a story with a recently taken photograph of the fifty-eight-year-old dad and his two other daughters. Not only did Lisa, thirty-one, spot her dad in the photo but she realised she was in the picture too. She said: "Me and my mum had been in the exact place where the picture was taken about a minute earlier and you can see us walking away. It is incredible."

What's in a name? In 1660, when a ship sank just off Dover the only survivor was a man called Hugh Williams. In 1767 another ship sank in the same spot, the sole survivor was a Mr Hugh Williams. Then in 1820, a ship capsized on the Thames. One man survived – Hugh Williams.

When a woman committed suicide after a failed relationship, her brother vowed revenge against Henry Ziegland, the man who had broken her heart. He produced a gun, shot at Ziegland but only injured him, with the bullet lodging in a nearby tree. Thinking he had killed him he turned the gun on himself. Years later, Henry was clearing that very land and used dynamite to remove the tree. The bullet, dislodged with considerable force, and shot out striking Ziegland, killing him instantly.

These three stories, I'm sure, would rouse the theorists, the dabblers in dark arts and the fate believers into a froth, but what have I learnt from these uncanny coincidences?

1. Don't call your son Mick if your surname is Dick.

2. If you're going on a boat trip, change your name to Hugh Williams.

3. You don't blow up trees – you cut them down.

~~

Today, I've decided, is badger day. I am going to badger the realtors in no uncertain terms to find us somewhere to live in this city. They are going to get up off their *asses* and work. That doesn't sound right, does it? I'm going to have to ask someone of substance over here why they insist on confusing the splendid English word "arse" with a pack animal. Giving someone a kick up the donkey just doesn't have the same impact somehow.

Anyway, I digress. I eventually got an appointment to view an apartment later in the morning with Jeroen, a softly spoken young guy who was born and raised in Amsterdam. As a matter of fact New York, as you probably know, began its life as New Amsterdam. Feeling in a generous mood, Holland granted an area of land in the Hudson River Valley to the Dutch West India Company in 1621. Manhattan Island was part of that area and was founded three years later and given the name of New Amsterdam. Only in 1664, when seized by us pillaging English, was it divided into two colonies and named New York and New Jersey.

Enlightened with this knowledge I sprang out of bed and pulled back the heavy-duty curtains to look out of my eighth storey hotel window. I was greeted by snowflakes, the size of a baby's fists, falling past my naked body at a disturbing rate. Not the ideal day to trudge around the city that never sleeps looking for somewhere warm to, well, sleep. But it had to be done. I dressed in a manner that I hoped would withstand the elements.

I left the hotel with a sizeable, woolly scarf wrapped around my face and baseball cap pulled down to the bridge of my nose – if I can't find somewhere to live at least I can rob a bank. I had to walk down two blocks and across six avenues to reach my destination. The wind was almost horizontal, forcing the snow into my eyes and making them sting, but the novelty of walking along the streets of Manhattan made me feel like a child who had been allowed out on his own for the first time.

I felt daring, intrepid even, as I weaved my way between the multi-cultural characters all wrestling with the invasive conditions. Beneath my scarf, which was now very damp and starting to tickle my nose and lips, I wore a stupid grin on my face. I was confident that I was the only pedestrian smiling in this atrocious weather. Why? 'Cos I was an Englishman in New York.

Although, I have to say, it was frustrating having to stop every hundred yards or so to wait for the all-powerful red hand to turn to white, which in turn stops the endless flow of vehicles (mainly yellow taxis). This was my invitation to cross each of the numerous intersections within the network that was Manhattan. If your timing was off it could take an age to cover a relatively short distance. The plus side, of course, was that it was a simple system to negotiate and remember.

The avenues, thirteen in all, ran from north to south of the island and the streets, over one hundred and fifty, from east to west. All the avenues, apart from three, were numbered in sequence as were all the streets. It was not the most romantic way of labelling the once capital city of America (1785–1790) but it was impossible to get lost. I could have learnt the New York taxi drivers' "knowledge" in my coffee break.

I met Jeroen at the apartment and was immediately impressed. He wore a pencil-lead-grey suit, shiny black brogues and white starched shirt. His paisley tie, which I thought went out with tanktops and penny collars, was not the coolest way to finish off the ensemble. Still, I overlooked this deficiency of good taste as he had a firm handshake and a winning smile, but it was the apartment that delivered the best impression.

The front of the building consisted of a heavy oak door surrounded by large plate-glass windows – all very grand. Inside stood a concierge who, on our arrival, unlocked and opened the door for us. The first thing I noticed was that he was very erect and smartly dressed. The second thing I noticed was that it was Lionel Ritchie – I swear. The resemblance was quite unnerving. The curly black hair, the long chin, toothy smile, the whole package.

There were two concierges, I found out later, one for the day shift and one for the night shift. Lionel was on the latter, his duty being from ten p.m. to ten a.m. How appropriate, I thought, that he should work *all night long*. And what a wonderful surprise; the city of New York had at last done us proud. To make up for the rude hotel staff and Aubrey the arsey waiter, they had arranged for America's biggest soul singing star to look after us. Lionel went on to be a good friend during our stay.

The lobby was well furnished with two plush sofas and an oak desk for the concierge. Great start. As soon as the door to the apartment was opened I knew I would take it.

As I entered the open-plan hallway there were two steps down to the sitting room which was large and square. It contained a sizeable TV, mahogany writing desk, dining table and two plump, deep-red leather sofas. The bedroom was of the same dimensions and housed a queen-sized bed. The kitchen and bathroom were just about big enough for their uses. The entire flat had varnished, honey-coloured oak floorboards and possessed a warm and comfy character. This was the one. Hang on! There must be a catch. The rent? No, we could afford it. Just. This was definitely the one.

I was on my mobile to Deb in a blink and she was at the apartment within twenty minutes. The rent was, in fact, a smidge over the limit of our budget but after a short discussion a deal was agreed for one month with the option of a further two. It was situated on East 55th Street between 1st and 2nd Avenue and was a respectful, safe area. This stretch of 2nd Avenue was bristling with pubs, wine bars and restaurants of all denominations.

In the evening, back in our hotel, we dined early and cheaply. Just after nine fifteen p.m., weary but possessed of sanguine spirit, we slid into our wafer-thin beds for the last time. Tomorrow we were going to feel like we belonged here.

Chapter Five

My job today, whilst my wife was at work, was to transfer me, four suitcases, a guitar and golf clubs from a characterless hotel to a cool apartment. Champing at the bit, I rang Jeroen at nine thirty a.m. No answer. New York realtors will never die from being over industrious that's for sure. I left a message on his answerphone.

With a frustrated sigh I lay on my bed, surrounded by mountains of luggage, staring at the wall. I looked at my watch every three and a half minutes as if by doing so it would force Jeroen to pick up his phone and ring me. An hour later and I was sound asleep, mouth open, dribbling and dreaming of licking the white froth of a Brooklyn Brown from the breasts of a naked and well proportioned Irish barmaid.

I was in the middle of my best dream for years as my mobile yelped into life, scaring the life out of me.

'Hi, Mr. Sullivan, it's Jeroen. I just got in and picked up your message. Everything appears to be in place. I just need you to sign some forms and, of course, I require a cheque from you. When could you come over?'

'An hour ago, Jeroen.'

''Scuse me?'

'I'll be there before you can put the phone down.'

So, I zipped out of my hotel, hailed one of the three million taxis passing by and arrived at his company's address just after eleven a.m. The facia of the building was a donkey-brown coloured rough stone and appeared to be quite old.

Inside the arched entrance hall I came face-to-face with one of those quaint, ancient elevators that you have to pull the concertina-type metal gate across to enter. The gate weighed a ton but I managed to get it open wide enough for me to squeeze inside. I popped two veins in my neck pulling it back again and pressed the 4th floor button. Nothing happened. I pressed again – dick all, rien, not a twitch.

'Why?' I asked the elevator politely. I pulled the gate back once again and, with wide stance and clenched buttocks, slammed it shut slicing a substantial layer of skin from two knuckles in the process. 'Ouch! Fucking thing! With all the money I'm paying this fucking company they could at least provide a lift from the twentieth-fucking-century.' I was cursing out loud to myself now as blood began to seep from my throbbing fingers.

I placed my freshly peeled pinkies into my mouth and pressed the button marked four with my elbow and the platform beneath me shuddered and began to move slowly upwards. Ah! At least I was moving in the right direction, but the trouble was that everything was moving – me, the floor, the walls and the ceiling. It was as if the mechanism suffered from cerebral palsy.

After an hour, I passed the first floor. A middle-aged lady with large hair was walking past on the landing and threw me a weird look. It said, 'Why are you using that ridiculous elevator? You're gonna die!' She disappeared behind a glass-panelled office door from which there now came the sound of collective giggling. This was not good; I had three more floors to go and I wondered if I would reach my destination before nightfall.

As I passed the third floor the elevator jumped, clanked, shuddered and stopped. The decrease in the upward velocity of my body was minimal but it soon dawned on me that I was now completely stationary. I say stationary in the sense that I wasn't going up or down, but this vintage hoist was now rocking to and fro against the sides of the lift shaft whilst emitting a squealing sound. You know the sound – it's the one a rope makes when it's carrying too much weight. It was a touch worrying.

'Oh great! This is getting better by the second.' I gurgled. I pressed the four button again. No response. I pressed it harder – as if that was going to make any difference. The elevator refused to budge. After scanning the dimly lit, drab interior I noticed there was a small silver stud above my head. I prayed it would be an alarm bell. It was, thank goodness. I pressed it long and loud. After a few minutes the first floor lady with the hair reappeared on the stairs in between the 3rd and 4th floors. She now wore a "I told you so" smirk all over her face.

'Jump up and down. That should get it moving again.'

'Sorry?'

'Jump up and down.'

'Madam, I am dangling from a two hundred-year-old piece of knackered twine struggling to support an archaic piece of rusty shit, eighty feet above a concrete floor, and you want me to jump up and down. Are you completely mad?'

'That's the only way you're going to get her to move, honey.'

Ah! So, this caged prison had a gender. It was a woman. A very old and stubborn woman. This explained a lot.

'Are you sure that's the only way?'

'Trust me already!' she said with folded arms pushing up her ample bosom. I amazed myself that I could still lock onto a woman's thrusting breasts whilst my life hung by a thread – literally. Already? Why should I trust this sardonic stranger? Her expression had now turned to one of impatience.

'Right,' I mumbled to myself. I was not going to let this lady think I was a pitiful English coward so I jumped – a little bit.

'No, not like that. Like this.' She launched herself upwards and landed back down on the step heavily with a thump, her breasts very nearly tumbling out of her v-neck jumper and taking an age to return to a becalmed state. At least if I was to meet an unfortunate and messy death, I would go to my maker with the lasting image of those dancing boobies jiggling in a manner that only tits of a certain magnitude can jiggle.

'If I plummet three and a half floors to my death, tell my partner Deborah that I love her and to beat you around the head with a baseball bat.' With that, I jumped up as high as my legs could take me and landed with a crash. The elevator gave a squeak, a fart and once more set off on its painful ascent the remaining few yards to floor number four and safety. I pulled back the gate, quickly vacated my chamber of horrors and entered Jeroen's office.

'Ah, Mr. Sullivan,' said Jeroen as he got up from his desk and sauntered over. 'No problems finding us?'

'No. No problems at all. Oh, apart from nearly dying in your fucking lift.'

The colourful language took him by surprise. 'Ah! I should've told you about the elevator. So that was you ringing the alarm bell?'

'Oh, you heard it then?'

'Yeh. It sounds off all the time,' he said with a small snigger. 'It didn't bother you, did it?'

'Of course not,' I lied. 'Have you ever thought of getting someone in to fix it?' I offered, heavy with sarcasm.

'Er, no, actually. I suppose we should?'

My ironic tone was completely lost on him and that was his unexpurgated reaction to his client's flirtation with death.

He then showed me into a huge, cream painted waiting room filled with rows of desks and chairs similar to that of a school classroom. We sat at the back. I noted that everything in the States was so much larger than in England. If an estate agent back home had the luxury of a waiting room, which is doubtful, it would be the size of a broom cupboard. In actual fact, it would *be* the broom cupboard.

Jeroen laid before me reams of paperwork that needed to be read and signed.

'Ooh! Do you wanna plaster for those knuckles, Mr Sullivan?' he said, fearful that my blood loss may cause me to pass out, thus losing his commission.

I waved my good hand at him to indicate that I was fine and started to scan the volume of documents, which appeared to be a tad less bulky than the Magna Carta. After thirty seconds my temples started to constrict, my eyes glazed over and I lost the will to live. So, I quickly signed at all the places marked by a cross and handed over a big fat cheque for the first month's rent.

'Great! I won't keep you long,' Jeroen said, studying the cheque with dilated pupils and a hungry expression. It was at that moment that he reminded me of a ravenous lion who had just brought down a gazelle and was about to devour its prize. I thought at one point he was going to start licking the cheque. He disappeared from the room.

As Jeroen exited, a rotund American gentleman was ushered into the room by a very masculine looking woman with hair that resembled a baboon's arse – crinkly and possessed of many different colours. She looked at me as if she wanted to cut off my penis and departed. This guy was a sight to behold. It was ten below outside and he was wearing a massive short-sleeved Hawaiian shirt, ivory and silver striped linen trousers and brown sandals with… socks. Even worse… luminous green socks. He struggled in carrying armfuls of impressive looking photography equipment and proceeded to set up his gear in silence. As I watched, I was thinking maybe this was Jeroen's first sale and he'd arranged to have the happy moment caught on camera.

Suddenly, he looked over at me as though he'd just realised he was not alone. 'Hi, my name's Todd.'

'Hi, Todd. I'm Chris.' I got up, walked over and shook a dangling hand which was disagreeably limp and moist.

'Gee, you from England?'

'Only if you're not from the tax department.' He took a moment to realise I was not being serious. They're definitely not big on irony out here.

'Huh, you English and your sense of humour. I've just returned from England. I do quite a bit of work there. In fact, I got my first big break in the UK. When Richard Branson first started up Virgin Airlines, I did a big photo shoot with him for the American market.'

'Really, what's he like?'

'Gee, he's a real swell guy.'

A real swell guy! This was great. I didn't think people actually spoke like this outside of the film world. It was like meeting a fat, effeminate John Wayne. He went on to regale me with many interesting tales of all the celebs he had captured on film. Whether they were true or false was of no matter because I found myself really enjoying this flamboyantly dressed, eccentric's company.

Eventually Jeroen came back into the room. 'Here's your contract and your keys,' he announced proudly. Handshakes and smiles all round. He had his commission and we had somewhere to live.

'Goodbye, Jeroen; thanks for everything. Oh! And I think I'll take the stairs this time.' I turned to the storytelling snapper, 'Goodbye, Todd, nice to meet you. Small piece of advice, Toddy old son – dump the socks.' I didn't actually say that last bit but I think he got the message by the way I stared at his ludicrous feet on my departure.

I cabbed it back to the hotel, euphoria dripping from every pore, and checked out. I tipped the bellboy for taking four tons of baggage down in the elevator, tipped the taxi driver for helping me to move it into the foyer of my new apartment and tipped the concierge for helping me get said bags up to my first-floor flat. Expensive business this moving lark.

Alone, I closed the door behind me, hung all our clothes in the bedroom wardrobe and sat down on our shiny burgundy sofa which I now realised was not real leather. I looked around me and, for the first time since arriving in New York, felt totally at ease. That was until it dawned on me that we had no provisions in our small but perfectly formed kitchen.

So, I ventured out towards a nearby mini-supermarket only to see a sign outside Murphy's Irish pub announcing that last night's Champions League match, Chelsea versus Stuttgart, was being shown on cable TV inside. I didn't know the result so in I went. I ordered a pint of Guinness and introduced myself to the barman. His name was also Sullivan (Kieran). This could be dangerous.

Chelsea scraped a 1-0 win with an own goal from a generous German defender who, unfortunately, had tied his boots to the wrong feet. Two hours later, me and two pints of Guinness, admirably abstemious in the circumstances I thought, left the pub. I got the shopping, bought a bunch of lilac tulips and walked home. With food in the fridge, soap in the bathroom and flowers on the sitting room table it really did feel like home. When Deb arrived back from work her face, which was already looking younger, was a picture. To celebrate we went back to Murphy's and spent another hour in the charming company of Kieran. Us Sullivans have got to stick together.

Here is another strange fact. English pubs in general are probably the best in the world – not that I'm biased. The lighting is subtle, the décor is welcoming and most are filled with old beams, exposed brick and loaded with history and character. But, these days, the bar staff in England are either very young, lazy, foreign, amateurish or all of the aforementioned. This is because they are part-time, poorly trained and badly paid.

Sadly, the majority of pubs in The USA don't have that history; that ambience; that "je ne sais quoi". But, here's the rub: the American bartenders are nearly all full-time, well-trained, personable and utterly professional. I am aware that they are working for tips to boost their salary but give me a hard working, on-the-ball, polite, personable bar jockey who knows their job any day. I'd be far more relaxed and content and gladly buy them a drink. Surely, what other reasons are there to frequent an alehouse if not to chill out, get good service and be able to put the world to rights with a friendly face from behind the jump.

Deb and I finished off the evening with a cheeseburger apiece and were in bed by ten p.m. A peaceful first night in our new home – or so I thought.

At four in the morning we were woken by a raving lunatic in our bedroom banging on the radiator with a monkey wrench. 'What the ff...?' I sat up and looked around the room. When the noise repeated itself I realised that the heating system had come on and the radiators were in desperate need of a good bleeding. Not a great start for the first night in our East Side residence – surely, it can only get better.

I was wrong. A few hours after I had managed to relax back into semi-consciousness there was a cry from the bathroom of 'Urgh! Chris!' I leapt out of bed and rushed to my distressed wife expecting... well, I don't know what I was expecting. 'What the hell is this?' she asked, pointing to her feet.

Oh dear! Not only was the bath not draining the shower water away but six inches of someone else's grimy crud had floated up to join her and lap menacingly against her smooth and shapely calves.

'Yuk!' I said in sympathy. I was straight on the phone at nine a.m. to customer services. The phone rang and rang and rang – silly me – who's going to be awake at this ungodly hour?

At eleven a.m., I finally got to moan at someone. One hour later, an Hispanic looking gentleman with an enormous plunger arrived and succeeded to shift five inches of liquid shit below the level of our plughole. Whilst he was there I thought I'd take the opportunity to mention the banging pipes. This courteous complaint was met with the blankest of blank looks. He didn't appear to speak English. Here we go again.

My first thought when we knew we were going to live in a foreign country was, at least we won't have any language problems with the locals. How wrong could I be? I went through a hand signal and mime performance that Marcel Marceau would have been proud of until he finally comprehended my dilemma. Sadly, the diminutive handyman followed this with a shrug of his shoulders that said 'So what's the problem?'

After I took him by his grubby collar and banged his head against the radiator for a few minutes I think he began to understand my point. He promised to get the matter sorted, picked up his plunger and walked out the door swearing in a foreign tongue.

It was not yet midday and I felt exhausted. Lack of sleep and Jose the Hispanic handyman had taken their toll. I decided to watch a bit of golf on the cable TV golf channel and relax. When I turned the set on I discovered that I couldn't get the golf channel. Worse still, I couldn't get cable TV. Back on to customer services. Two hours later a chubby bloke wearing a baseball cap, button-popping gingham shirt and denims that revealed three inches of hairy bottom crack arrived, fiddled with the TV and said, 'Doesn't seem to be anything wrong, buddy.'

'Ah good! Cable's working now is it?'

'Oh! You're having problems with your cable. I thought it was your TV. I don't really know much about TV's to be honest.'

'Sorry? Who are you then?' I asked, in a manner that contained a sonorous ring of discontent.

'I look after most of the electrics for these apartments. Don't really do TV's.'

'So they've sent the wrong man to do the job?' I added, incredulous. 'Still, it must be difficult for customer services to identify TV man from man who knows bugger all about TV's. I've been in this not inexpensive flat, apartment, condo whatever you want to call it for less than twenty-four hours – the plumbing's knackered, the telly's knackered and the two blokes who have turned up to put it right know precious little about either function. Is it because I am English or does everyone in his country receive this treatment?'

The man, whose left eye had now developed a worrying twitch, apologised profusely, promised to sort it out and promptly exited. If he'd had a tail it would have been firmly tucked between his legs. I have to admit that shortly after his departure I felt somewhat guilty at venting my spleen upon his narrow, checked shoulders – but really! I loved this apartment and its location but I was getting increasingly narked about these frustrating encumbrances and ill-equipped tradesmen.

After all this excitement I needed to clear my head, get out of the apartment and see more of this city. I phoned Deb and arranged to meet her for lunch. I slipped on my shoes, threw on a jumper and warm coat and released myself out into the metropolis. Outside, I was confronted by a bitterly cold but beautiful day. As I took the ten-minute walk to her office, a huge, concordant sun shone down upon me from an unsullied sky. Despite the fact that it had to lean over enormous skyscrapers and peek through the sporadic gaps that had survived the city developers, it lifted my heart.

Deb only had an hour for lunch so we slipped into the nearest pasta joint. I was so pleased to see her that, on entering, I didn't take in my immediate surroundings. The place was cheaply furnished, dimly lit and felt grubby. My feelings of unease were not allayed any, after the waiter delivered our meals. On his way back to the kitchen, he proceeded to delve the two longest fingers of his left hand deep into the crevice of his baggy, denim covered buttocks causing him to walk like Robert Mitcham.

I turned to Deb, 'When the waiter comes back I must remember to apologise for eating while he was scratching his arse!' I looked at my greasy meal of spaghetti bolognaise and spent the next ten minutes pushing it around the plate. Deb did the same. Our whole conversation revolved around our surroundings and the two plates of what looked like diarrhoea swimming in half a pint of bicycle oil. This was not good.

I'd done enough complaining for the day so I left a twenty dollar bill under my plate, to cover the two meals, and we departed. After a brief walk around the area we bought two sandwiches from a small café, kissed and said our goodbyes.

On the way up to meet Deb, I had passed a gymnasium and we had talked briefly during lunch about joining. So, on my return journey, I went in and enrolled both of us into the sweat-filled workhouse. I managed to negotiate a very good three-month deal with Carl the blonde-haired, muscle-bound Apollo. My one hour induction was booked for the following morning. This would enable us to keep fit whilst our bodies struggled to cope with the extra booze and greasy pasta dishes that would inevitably be part of our sojourn.

Later that evening I popped out to get a Chinese takeaway for twenty dollars. When I opened up the bag in our snug kitchen, I found enough food to feed a small African village. As we eyed the Desperate Dan proportions on our plates, I said, 'This is too much for twenty dollars!' and realised immediately that this was a phrase I would never utter again in my lifetime.

The UK is home to approximately seven thousand Chinese takeaways and, from what I've seen so far, the citizens of New York City have also embraced this easy to eat fare (they call it a "carry-out") with a similar enthusiasm. What I would like to know is when, in China, the Chinese go down the pub for a few sherbets and can't be bothered to cook an evening meal are they tempted to get an English takeaway – or perhaps a Yankee carry-out. 'Sorry I'm a bit late luv; had a few games of mah-jong and a couple of beers with the lads down the Dog and Crispy Fried Duck, but I've brought home an English for you and the kids.'

Yep, I can see that working.

At least our in-house hi-fi system was not broken so we ploughed through our carry-out monster meal with the musical accompaniment from two of our cd's that we had brought over from the UK. I cordially invited Norah Jones and Frank Sinatra (when in Rome) into our sitting room to mollify my somewhat inharmonious day. They didn't let me down.

It was a minute after five thirty a.m. when I was woken by the 'pipe' band – the temptation beckons to write a song to the syncopated rhythm. In truth, I am not at all happy. I want to rename New York – *the city that never allows you to sleep.*

~~

I arrived at my new gym at eight thirty a.m. and slipped into my workout gear that, I've just realised, was probably the bee's knees when I last wore it in 1991. Also, I noticed that the body inside had lost its sleek and honed dimensions. Never mind, I was comforted by the fact that I still looked better than the old lady on the walking machine next to me. She was wearing a John McEnroe headband and a pink leotard that was struggling to contain a bum acting as ballast and which hovered three inches above her calf muscles.

As I was building up a controlled head of steam a young woman bearing the smile of a Hollywood actress approached me: five feet three, ginger hair and freckles and as fit as a butcher's. Aye, aye! Maybe I don't look so bad after all, I thought, doing my best to return the smile.

'Hi, my name's Shona and I'm your instructor,' she said, with a sudden air of authority. She had approached me, not because my infectious masculinity had arrested her attention, but to give me an hour's instruction on how to use the exercise machines in a correct and safe manner.

She started me off with ten minutes on the bike – realised after only three minutes that I was wearing a look of smugness so adjusted the setting to "OK, see how that feels smartarse" level. I threw her a devil-may-care smile and spent the next seven minutes pretending to be young and fit. When my time was up she led me off to the stair climbing apparatus. I followed like Bambi taking his first steps in life. Luckily, Shona didn't turn around.

This carried on for another forty-five minutes – her being energetic and eager, me pretending to be bullet-proof. Actually, I used to train and play heaps of sports, so my brain was very swiftly back in tune. Sadly, the body had forgotten the words.

After sixty, mostly painful, minutes I thanked Shona's freckly face and headed for a hot shower. My journey back to the flat was surprising in so far as the pavements seemed a good deal longer and had turned to sand. To avoid seizing up I thought it best to keep active. I decided to wash all our dirty clothes in the in-house laundry which, I was informed by Lionel Ritchie, was in the basement of our building. The weekly washing was a task forced upon me as a nine-year-old, after my mother died, and the aversion to the unwanted chore has never left me. But Deb was working full-time so it was a must-do.

I descended the concrete stairs deep into the bowels of the apartment block, carrying my basket full of washing, turned the wrong way and blundered into the janitor's room. He was watching baseball on his small TV. He had this look of guilt spread all over his little round face for some reason, but, after realising my mistake, he led me, via a complex of Colditz-like tunnels, to the laundry room and then departed. What Lionel forgot to tell me was that all the machines were "special credit card" operated. Also, there was no washing powder dispenser. Bugger!

I tried to retrace my steps back to the stairs and ended up in the janitor's room once again. I think he was beginning to suspect that I was the time and motion man checking up on his hours of work.

'Apparently, I need a special credit card to operate the washing machine,' I told him.

The janitor stood up from his chair and, remarkably, didn't get any taller. 'Eh?' he said, in a heavy Mexican bandit brogue that reminded me of that splendid film The Good, the Bad and the Ugly.

'I... need... special... credit card... for washy washy,' I spelt out, holding up my latticed container of slightly soiled garments in front of this swarthy individual. He nodded and issued me with a plastic laundry card stacked up with twenty dollars' worth of cleansing points. 'Oh, and I need washing liquid and fabric softener,' I said, forgetting to speak slowly.

His eyes narrowed, his lips tightened, his jaw expanded. A hairy hand rose slowly and stopped level with my solar plexus. He turned and as he reached behind his TV I was expecting him to pull out a gun. Instead, he produced a plastic cup full of washing powder and grinned for the first time, showing more gaps than teeth. I was so relieved to still be alive that I didn't push it for the conditioner.

After the washing machine had finished I loaded the wet washing carefully into a tumble drier and inserted my card. Nothing happened. Oh good! After five minutes of pressing buttons and kicking the machine (luckily no-one else was around) I realised it was out of order. I had to take it all out again and throw it into the one opposite. Bingo! I returned forty five minutes later and took the basket full of clean, dry, virtually crease-free clothes back to our apartment feeling very pleased with myself. As I was unloading the basket in imperious fashion it suddenly struck me how sad I was to be thrilled about the state of our freshly laundered apparel.

When Deb arrived home and saw all the clean clothes folded on our bed she was beside herself. And so was I. It was worth all the hassle after all – just.

~~

Saturday and Deb's first visit to the gym. Her instructor mysteriously did not turn up. No matter, I showed her all that I was taught yesterday and we both had a good workout. There were no muscle-bound posers present today so we both felt fairly comfortable in our somewhat alien surroundings. I could feel the booze flowing out of my pores as I pounded inexorably towards the TV screen on the wall that was showing a baseball game. When I think of it, every time I've turned on a television in this country the station has always been showing a baseball game.

It was another stunning blue-sky day and the temperature had risen from 32°F in midweek to a hard to believe 54°F, making New York appear ship-shape and shiny. On the way back to our flat we stopped off at the Food Emporium, which was a rather elaborate name for a small and under-stocked supermarket, to do the serious shop for the coming week. We discovered that most of the brand names were different from those in the UK but managed to pick out what we thought was safe and would taste nice by the colours on the packaging and shaking or squeezing the goods therein.

Just as we were about to cart eight heavy bags of shopping across four blocks to our apartment, the smiling checkout woman said, 'Would you like those delivered, sir?' Music to our Anglian ears. Unladen, we strolled back to our abode and ten minutes later a large, finely-honed man arrived with our goods. He was the most charming gentleman I had met in this city to date. He deposited all the fat bags of shopping in a neat line in our small kitchen and I deposited five dollars into his enormous hand. I'm beginning to like this place.

Deb, who was now in serious shopping mode, fancied adding to her restricted travelling wardrobe. So we walked up to 5th Avenue to the world of Saks, Macy's and Armani. There were some excellent bargains to be had. I have heard of people flying over from England to scoop up armfuls of designer labels for a fraction of their London prices and remain quids in, despite the cost of the same day return plane flight ticket.

Most stores were very modern in their appearance but Saks Fifth Avenue had a more European feel. The business was founded in 1867 by Andrew Saks (not to be confused with the esteemed British actor with a similar sounding name who

71

played the wonderful Manuel in Fawlty Towers). This was an older building with towering ceilings and wood-panelled walls. The interior was classic, the ambience cool sophistication and, yes, the prices were cheaper than those back home.

With new garments in hand and now feeling shopped-out we got a cab back to our apartment.

As Deb started to prepare the veg for our evening meal, she turned to me. 'Why don't you have a nice hot bath before dinner, darling?'

What a lovely woman and what a champion idea! I ran a deep, lemon-fragranced bath and just as I sank back into bubbly, liquid heaven all hell broke loose as a brain-bursting siren filled the apartment. 'What the...' I spluttered.

Deb rushed into the bathroom. I could see her mouth moving but couldn't hear a word she was saying. I raised myself up from my position of foamy comfort to just about make out an 'Oh bugger! Chris. I've set the fire alarm off.' Apparently, the oven had overheated, causing a billow of fatty smoke to crawl up the walls thus triggering a screaming fire alarm, which was screwed to the sitting room ceiling.

'Sod it!' I said, as it quickly dawned on me that, as a man, I was supposed to sort out all-known mechanical problems. I climbed out of the bath dripping wet and, still naked, pulled out a dining chair, climbed up and attempted to disable the eardrum-shredding appliance. Deb was now standing next to me laughing at the sight of my nakedness and the large blob of foam clinging to the end of my manhood making it look very similar to an ice-cream cone. A 99 it wasn't. Perhaps a 33.

Whilst I struggled, for an age, to disconnect the wilful, tight-fitting battery, on tiptoes and upon shaky platform, Deb stripped off behind my back and jumped in the bath. My bath! Unbelievable. I ended up peeling the spuds (carefully) in the nude. It was not a sight to warm the heart.

The steak meal was worth waiting for, though, going some way to make up for a traitorous wife and me having to put up with seconds in a barely warm de-bubbled bath.

I don't know from where the Yanks source their steaks, but they are big, tender and delicious.

~~

A quick look at the diary that had travelled with me from the UK told me it was that odd date, that extra day wedged in every four years, which rather spoils an otherwise orderly and well-formulated Gregorian calendar – the 29th February. If the forever realigning equinox would only stop fidgeting about we wouldn't need this clumsy addition. But as it fell on a blue-skied Sunday I was determined that we were going to enjoy this chronological quirk.

It was 56°F and the weather was pleading with us to explore more of this city. We decided to check out downtown so we took a cab to 8th Street and 2nd Avenue to East Village and headed west along 8th. Manhattan can be many different things to many people, but there is one thing that it's not: it is never boring. Each quarter has its own personality where the environment and its inhabitants differ quite noticeably from their neighbours. The street here was lined with small, mysterious looking shops that all opened out onto the pavement – all a bit Harry Potter.

As we continued west, we found ourselves walking past some very strange looking individuals. It seemed that the fabric of leather appeared to be the only material available to wear in this part of town. What's more, it was not in great supply as everyone was wearing it at least one size too small.

When we reached Greenwich Village we appeared to have passed through a time-warp. Here, the town folk all seemed to have been sucked back into the seventies. Flared trousers, flowery shirts and Cuban heels assailed us from every angle. Did I actually wear this offence to fashion? Surely not.

"The Village", as it is known amongst the locals, was the bohemian capital of New York in the late-nineteenth to mid-twentieth centuries. If you were not an artist, sculptor or musician you were in the minority in this cool part of town. However, due to the extraordinary rise in the cost of property in the sector, the artistically bent but perennially broke all had to move out to smoke their pot and create their masterpieces in cheaper digs. The residents in this part of town now comprised mainly of upper middle-class families. It was a great source of entertainment, though, to witness the outlandish garb on display and the strutting dudes attempting to preserve the bygone tradition of the area.

After turning a few more corners we found what we'd been looking for – a street full of shoe shops. How dear Imelda would have loved it here. I've lusted after a pair of cowboy boots, nothing flashy mind, since I was sixteen years of age, but never found a pair to fit over my high instep. After visiting every blooming shop and trying to squeeze into over a hundred pairs of boots, I could not find one pair that fitted. Not one. I felt robbed. Now I know how the ugly sisters must have felt.

Feeling downhearted we forged ahead, my spirits lifted by the sight of Fiddlesticks. Yes, you've guessed it – an Irish bar. This one was different, however; it was moody, full of nooks and crannies, with scarred oak-panelled walls the colour of burnt toast. Tucked away on different levels were dimly-lit rooms hidden behind tired, burgundy and asparagus-green curtains, hung carelessly from brass poles. This was old Irish meets Dickens. I was entranced.

As we approached the bar to the squeak of well-trodden, burnished floorboards my eyes separated in all directions. Distressed-wood cabinets with glass-fronted doors stood in murky corners; some packed with old leather-bound books, some containing strange-shaped bottles advertising creams and potions from days of old. On closer inspection, these medicinal vessels claimed to cure glue ear, lumbago, chronic diarrhoea and just about everything else you wouldn't choose to have.

Either side of bare-bricked arches hung old violin cases and sepia photos of scary, stern-faced Irish folk that hung menacingly above grandfather clocks and antique lamps. To keep in with the ambience of the hostelry I ordered two pints of mead and an opium pipe and sat down with my wife at a scarred oak table opposite Bill Sikes, Bull's-eye and Nancy. It was a spooky yet entertaining episode.

~~

The experience of travelling back in time within the walls of the thought-provoking Fiddlesticks bar had a lasting effect on my brain. Instead of tumbling forward to the present, I began dipping into the early beginnings of NYC.

The first known native "New Yorkers" were the Lenape, also known as the Delaware Indians, who hunted and farmed in the area between the Delaware and Hudson rivers. They named it Manna-hata, which means island of many hills. It was only at the beginning of the 16th century that Europeans began to explore the region. None actually settled there until 1624 when the Dutch West India Company sent thirty families to live and work in a tiny settlement, now known as Governors Island.

Two years later the settlement's Governor General, Peter Minuit, purchased the much larger Manhattan Island from the natives offering trade goods, the equivalent of sixty guilders, in return. These goods consisted mainly of tools, cloth and farming equipment. That sounds like a pretty shrewd deal to me. Old Pete sure knew a good bargain when he saw one.

'Thanks for the lovely big island. Here's a plough, some shovels and a bundle of old shirts and trousers that I've grown out of. Enjoy! Oh, and if you could all move out by Friday afternoon!'

When the settlement moved to what was now called New Amsterdam, the population was less than three hundred. In 1664, the future King James II (the Duke of York), aware that this location was now a thriving trading post, sent out four warships to seize the land. The Dutch, apparently having no heart for a battle, gave up the island without a drop of blood being spilt.

'Well, that was easy,' I can hear the Duke declare on hearing the news. So, victorious and bursting with pride, he plumped up his royal ego and renamed it New York. By 1760, the area of New York City had grown to eighteen thousand inhabitants. Surpassing Boston, this was now the second largest city in the American colonies after Philadelphia. Five years later, with a population of 202,500, consisting mainly of immigrants from Europe and Africa, it became the largest city in the Western Hemisphere.

✝ It was at the turn of the 20th century that New York City became the area we know today. In 1895, the residents of The Bronx, Queens, Staten Island and Brooklyn – all independent cities at the time – voted to consolidate with Manhattan to form a five borough Greater New York.

Having said all this, New York City is almost like several cities in one with many divisions amongst its occupants. The five boroughs each have their own government operation within the city's broader government system and each has its own borough president with limited governing powers, plus its own culture and reputation, but it works. Today, more than eight million people live in the five boroughs and, for the most part, they seem a fairly happy lot. ✦

Chapter Six

Greig, the manager of the building, has finally responded with apologies and promises to my list of requests for pipes that don't go bang in the night, cable TV, cushions for the sofa, and a promised TV for the bedroom. But now, all of a sudden, my laptop cannot get internet connection no matter how much I threaten it. As I was making a much needed and relaxing cup of tea, Greig knocked on my door. It was ten a.m.

'I've been bleeding your pipes when you were out yesterday. Should be OK now,' he said confidently.

I replied that the bleeding pipes were still making an unholy racket at a time when only the milkman should be awake. He didn't get my play on words and didn't know what a milkman was. Sadly, I will have to come to terms with the undeniable fact that I have become a jabbering foreigner whilst speaking, primarily, the same language as my new hosts.

I tend to regard Americans as kind of distant relatives that have just fannied around with our means of communication – mainly by dropping the word subtle from their vocabulary and day-to-day lives. Nevertheless, I still welcome most of them into my bosom.

I guess it's the insularity of a great many Americans that I find hard to fall in love with. In my experience, most tend to have no idea where their next state is, let alone the geographical location of little damp England. Apparently, only

78

thirty-eight percent of Americans own a passport and if George W. Bush was one such stay-at-home, as was rumoured… well, need I say more?

Yes, I know it's a big country, but so is Australia and they have discovered that a world exists outside of their own territory. In fact, we can't move in the UK for hard-working, lager-swilling Aussies. That's not to say my Yankee hosts aren't industrious, just a tad blinkered.

Our apartment is slap bang next to the site of a new reach-for-the-sky construction, so there is quite a lot of drilling and sawing during the day. Every morning, when I leave the flat, I weave my way through chicaned scaffold poles and half a dozen or so friendly builders.

These workers, on first inspection, appear to be exactly the same as our UK counterparts – a tad overweight, a bit sweaty and chatty, and with baggy jeans that are ingeniously cut to display four inches of arse-crack. However, there are two obvious differences: the New York teams always appear to be doing something – working – and when they finish at three thirty p.m., they clean up their mess, sweep the thoroughfares, hose down the road and, would you believe, hose the muck off their lorries before going home. The site is well managed and generally neat and tidy. Joy.

Today, I bid a good morning to the friendly workmen, then wandered through a few streets and avenues, eventually stumbling across a hardware store not five minutes from where we live. My short journey was to buy two TV trays, from which to eat our evening meals, whilst perched on our voluminous, bottom-squeaky leatherish sofa. Why I should call them *TV* trays I'm not sure, because most of the broadcasted content, I've found, is pretty uninspiring. Game shows and soaps rule the waves in this part of the world. How I ache for a drama, a play, a credible crime thriller, a *University Challenge*, an *Only Fools and Horses*.

On the way back with my trays I took a slightly different route. I passed a shop that sold prints and paintings and inside I found a photograph of a racing yacht, pitching and swaying amidst an undulating and lively ocean. The thirteen man crew, all dressed in cool white onesies, looked as though they were all about to be tossed into the heaving, sun-spangled waves – the scene was exhilarating, full of action and daring. It made me feel as though I wanted to dash out and buy a sou'wester, run away to sea and chant salty seaman's shanties for the remainder of my life.

The shop owner introduced himself as Raoul and was tickled pink that I was from "London, England" and wanted to spend some of my money in his establishment. I left a small deposit and arranged to have the picture framed. If I don't find anything on US television to spark my interest, I'll watch the picture for three months.

At six p.m., I met Deb at the gym. Somehow she had lost both of our padlocks, which we were expected to supply, for our changing-room lockers. So, we had to tie up our doors with spare shoelaces I had in my bag. Despite our valuables not being totally secure, we were now feeling more at ease in the palace of perspiration.

After an hour, having left our Anglo-Saxon body fluids all over the state-of-the-art American exercise apparatus, we returned to our separate changing rooms. Despite our misgivings, our lockers were still intact. I'm not sure that would have been the case back home; a massive tick for New York.

To replace vital lost liquid we shimmied, for the first time, into PJ Clarke's, which was a great find. It had the look and feel of the Cheddar Cheese which is a cosy pub in a back alley off Fleet Street – a must do in London if you like your taverns full of wrap-around history and dripping with character.

PJ Clarke's was filled with suited and booted business men and women, sitting reading papers, standing in close circles debating economies, boasting of deals, discussing sport and the opposite sex. The background music of Sinatra and assorted crooners sat well in the nostalgic atmosphere. This was the place for us. Having spent an inordinate amount of time in London's city pubs this was a little bit of home from home.

The only slightly disconcerting aspect of the alehouse was the men's toilet. This consisted of a glass vestibule placed in a centralised position and directly opposite the bar. The door opened straight onto three very tall, old-fashioned, veiny, porcelain urinals, so at least one third of the merrymaking customers could watch you take a piss whenever someone entered or departed.

That wasn't the worst of it. The two cubicles for number two's were fitted with three-foot-long saloon bar doors, similar to those of old cowboy films. The sight of concertinaed trousers wrapped around thin, hairy legs and strained expressions on embarrassed faces was not the image I wanted to take back to my half-finished pint of Guinness.

Out of extreme necessity, I used the facility just once during my stay. Why New Yorkers are happy to turn their lavatorial habits into a performance for every Tom, Dick and Harriet to ogle is beyond me. The lack of privacy was such that I may as well have relieved myself in the corner of the bar. Astonishing behaviour, but a great talking point.

~~

I woke up this morning full of the joys of early March. After a relaxed breakfast and a cup of Lipton's tea, the only brand that appears to be available here, I skipped down the two flights of stairs in our apartment complex, wished Lionel a good morning and strode up 2nd Avenue to collect my yacht from the small picture shop.

It was ten past ten and still closed. Swipe me! Do New York businesses suffer from morning sickness? I wandered around aimlessly for twenty minutes and found myself back at our apartment. By way of wasting time, I tried to find a watchable TV programme amid the two hundred channels on my box whilst eating another bowl of Oat Crunch which was the only breakfast cereal I recognised in the Emporium. Aah! I found a programme I recognised on BBC America – it was an eight-year-old episode of *Ground Force*. Alan Titchmarsh looked about seventeen years old and Charlie Dimmock didn't even have a speaking part; she just did what she was good at, which was to show off her splendid, unfettered thrupennies. Actually, Titchmarsh, even as a squeaky-voiced stripling, was very engaging and knew his stuff. Charlie, a lovely gal, bless her, is one of those people on TV that sound more impressive when they keep quiet.

But even as I watched, my mind was bobbing about aboard my yacht. After two more repeats of Ground Force, I tore myself away from the TV and departed to collect my picture. Whoopee! It was open. Raoul, our flamboyant proprietor, dressed in baby-blue slacks and matching v-neck yakswool sweater, no shirt, no shoes, hairy chest and hairy feet, has done a sterling job with a matt black frame. I was just about to hand over thirty dollars, the agreed price, when he informed me that was the price without the tax. My face must have betrayed my inner feeling of consternation.

'That's the way they do it here, sweetheart,' he said, eyeing me in a fashion that bordered on sensual.

'So, why don't shopkeepers add on the tax before telling you the price of an item or service?' A shake of the head, an eyelash flutter and a 'You're in New York, darling,' was all I received back.

I had been told by the management when I moved in that I couldn't bang any nails into the walls of my apartment so I asked to buy an adhesive hook.

'That's one dollar,' he replied.

I waited for the addition of the levy but he stayed silent. No tax on adhesive hooks. Result! I paid him his dollars, wished him well and kissed him goodbye. I didn't really kiss him but I'm sure he would've been thrilled if I had.

On my return, I read the accompanying instructions which claimed to not take three layers of emulsion plus render off the wall when the tax-free hook is removed. I've seen these instructions before and don't trust them, so I decided I'm going to leave the hook in situ when we return to Blighty. I hung the cool picky on our previously forlorn wall at the end of our bed.

It looked the biz and in its small square way lent the room a sniff of adventure.

The gloom of six p.m. arrived, but my wife did not. I began to worry – New York is an enormous place and she is only five feet nine and a bit. The phone rang at six thirty p.m. I skidded, in my socks, across our shiny floor to answer it.

It was Deb. 'Sorry I'm late, darling. I've been interviewing the US members of staff, one by one, in an attempt to shake this lot up. I really need to improve morale and work rate at this place.'

'How'd it go?'

'All they did was to take turns in blaming each other for a lackadaisical, underachieving office. Honestly, Chris, I've witnessed more adrenalin in a hospital recovery room,' she concluded.

'Leadership and direction, that's what you're good at. You can do it,' I said. I then suggested the distribution of hand mirrors, so they could all take a good look at *themselves*.

Deb replied, 'On reflection, that's good advice.'

I told her, in no uncertain terms, that I did the jokes in this relationship and to hurry home safely. I just hoped she had time to instil these practices into the bevy of under-achievers during our two and a half months left on this island.

We stayed in tonight and watched four more episodes of Ground Force. I'm beginning to get a serious taste for this gardening lark. Later in bed, I drifted off to sleep and stepped straight into a horticultural dream where I was doing a two day "make-over" of Central Park with a topless Charlie Dimmock. The images of what we got up to were so vivid that when I woke in the morning next to Deb, I experienced a sharp pang of guilt. Quickly, I reassured my conscience with the thought that at least my erotic agricultural dream wasn't centred around a topless Alan Titchmarsh.

~~

My brother, Barry, rang me this morning on my mobile from London to berate me for not keeping in touch by email. I told him my laptop wasn't able to email, gmail or effing fmail. It had thrown a massive wobbly for no apparent reason. I think he believed me. Shortly afterwards Deb's boss rang from London. I told him the same story. He suggested I check the lead from the laptop to the phone socket (this was before wi-fi). 'Thanks, Tom,' I said, with a small titter. 'Yeah, OK, I'm not stupid, you know,' I wanted to say as I laid the phone back on its cradle.

I looked at my laptop with a puzzled frown. No, surely not... I unplugged the old lead from the machine and replaced it with the apartment phone lead and, blow me down with a feather, it worked like new. Why the original lead had stopped working in the space of a twelve hour trip to the states was mysterious to say the least.

I was taught as a kid that if something goes wrong with an electrical appliance, the first thing you check is the plug and supply lines to the power source. I felt very stupid, so I blamed Deb. Immediately, I sent an email to Barry with apologies. It must have appeared to him that I was making lame excuses and had just forgotten my communication duties. Oh well, he's four years older than me and boasts of always being the sensible one – so, no harm done there, then.

Right, I needed a new lead. I discovered, via Google, where the nearest computer shop was and proceeded to cart my laptop up six avenues and over two blocks to Comp USA on Broadway. The shop sign was in big red letters, the store was practical and unfriendly. I arrived on the first floor, which was just a bit smaller than a football pitch and accosted a young male assistant who was walking towards me. He had an enormous red face and was wearing a red and mauve uniform. He reminded me of a nasty bruise.

'Excuse me. I wonder if you can help me?'

The bruise eyed me as you would regard someone caught in the act of shagging a sheep. Wearing an over-exaggerated frown, he completely ignored my request and carried on past me.

''Scuse me! Do they train you to be rude or does it come naturally?' I said, as I turned to vent my spleen. I was about to chase after this discourteous fellow until I read the large yellow words on his back: *Gerry's Motors*. Whoops!

Eventually I found a service desk with someone who actually worked there. 'Hi,' I said to the middle-aged, crewcutted assistant, 'I need a new lead to plug into my personal computer, please.' He looked at me with a blank stare, as though I was speaking Swahili. 'I require a new lead?' I said, enunciating each word like a 1950s BBC announcer. I could see the guy was struggling to translate English into American. Clearly, the required intimacy with the origins of our language did not reside within his provincial skull. There was another embarrassing silence until I held the old lead up in front of his face and whipped him around the head with it. Well, that's what I wanted to do.

'Aha, you wanna another wire,' he told me, pronouncing the *r* four times, as Americans do. For pity's sake, have you no flexibility within your knowledge of the English language, I yearned to say. But I didn't. I soon learned that if you don't utter the exact wording in your sentences, which the inhabitants of this twenty-first century financial centre of America employ, you are too often greeted with glazed-eyed ignorance at best and utter disdain at worst. There appears to be no hint of elasticity in the vocabulary department of certain people here that the rest of us, from other English speaking countries, acquire along life's journey.

The Full Monty film, I am led to believe, was a big hit in the States. God only knows how they understood a word of the film's strong Sheffield brogue over here. Maybe they had subtitles.

As I zigzagged homeward my mild frustration was lifted by the unexpected meeting with the New York City Center on 55th Street between 6th and 7th Avenues. This delightful building, with its terracotta tile-encrusted dome, was Manhattan's first performing arts centre. Built in 1923, it was originally called the Mecca Temple by the Ancient Arabic Order of the Nobles of the Mystic Shrine, an appendant body to Freemasonry. Thank goodness someone had the bright idea of shortening their name to the Shriners.

After the financial crash of 1929, the Shriners were unable to pay the taxes on the property and it became city owned. It was in the early 1940s that it was decided to convert the building to a home for the performing arts. It opened its doors on 11th December 1943 to a concert by the New York

Philharmonic Orchestra. Countless star performers and Broadway musicals have and continue to grace its stage.

It was sights, such as this beautiful theatre, with their rich and inspiring histories, that suddenly put all the petty irritations of language and strange customs into perspective. New York City with its thriving assemblage of differing clans and ideals had much to offer its citizens and visitors such as myself. Refreshed, with head held aloft and a new wire in hand, I strode back home in a frame of mind befitting this weird and wonderful place.

~~

I woke this morning with one thought on my mind. Were we going to move or not? The one plus was that everything in the apartment seemed to be in place and working to an acceptable degree apart from those blasted pipes – my New York apartment's version of reveille. Could I be bothered to hunt the streets and avenues for another apartment, repack four suitcases, sign reams of forms and carp about more, inevitable, teething problems?

Annoyingly, though, there was a voice emanating from the rear portion of my head telling me that our perfect living quarters were out there, somewhere, waiting for me to discover. Amongst the steaming drains and lofty columns, I was convinced there was a bolt-hole with views over Manhattan to thrill and galvanise my artistic bent. I made the decision to jump on the internet train and have an electronic chug across this exciting city in search of Utopia.

Mid-search, my half-sister, Val, phoned on my mobile from Phoenix, Arizona expecting me to be in England. She got quite a shock to find that I was eating and drinking my way through the Big Apple, which sounds like every maggot's dream journey.

I am very remiss when it comes to keeping in contact with my relatives and she let me know it, deservedly, for *two hours*. Then, I remembered why I don't phone her as much as I should. To me, the pain of a two hour phone conversation is akin to affixing clothes pegs to my scrotum. The conversation was mentally exhausting for my small brain; not to mention that my right ear, by the end of the call, bore a remarkable resemblance to a sweaty, raw pork chop.

I had spent most of the day searching for another place to live only to find that everywhere else was either dingy, smaller or more expensive. I am still unsure whether or not to extend our one month contract at our apartment. The early morning racket seems to be unfixable. I've warned the management that, if it continues for much longer, I will turn off the radiators and start a fire with the furniture.

'You English and your sense of humour,' I heard for the second time in this country. I'm guessing this will not be the last time this phrase pops up before we do the swerve back to rain-sodden England.

When Deb arrived home at six thirty, she was carrying a small wrapped parcel. On seeing my raised eyebrows, she said, 'Shark steaks for tea.'

'Wow! Steaks... made out of shark!' I remarked, not sure whether I was excited or apprehensive. The presence of the crowned head of the underwater food chain sharing our apartment, well, two neatly-trimmed chunks of it, was food for thought. Another thought suddenly occurred to me: I was a man about to eat a man-eater!

As it turned out the predator tasted delicious but as I took my first bite on its meaty flesh I said, 'Now you know how it feels, you vicious beast.'

I had read Peter Benchley's wonderful but hair-raising book Jaws when it first appeared in our bookstores in 1974. I then put myself through it all again by watching Spielberg's excellent film some years later. Now the only close encounter, sharkwise, with which I feel comfortable is when it has recently passed on and a well-cooked chunk of it has been squeezed between four potatoes and a sprinkling of broccoli. Even then I don't feel totally safe.

Chapter Seven

We've been here for almost three weeks. Where did that go? The older I get the faster the days speed by. At this rate by the time I reach seventy I'll be eighty.

We have arranged to meet Deb's colleague Amy and her fiancé Ryan at a jazz club tonight. We had to eat first, however, so we rode on a cab down to Houston and La Guardia which is in the Soho area. It was first named in the nineteen seventies, taken from SOuth of HOuston and notable for being the location of artists and art galleries. During the day this part of New York had a reputation for hip restaurants and high-end boutiques.

But, this was night-time and I was not quite sure about this district as we alighted from our banana-coloured mode of transport. It had a dodgy, uncomfortable feel about it for some inexplicable reason. Maybe it was me.

After a short walk around the area, where I was looking backwards more than forwards we found a square goldfish bowl that served food. Most of the tables were full but there were two seats at the bar on which no bottoms were plonked – not for long. We squeezed in beside two Americans who, at first, seemed very friendly.

After initial introductions, they proceeded to launch straight into a lively dissertation on the merits of the Guggenheim Museum. I was informed that the museum was up on 88th and 5th and next to the Jackie Onassis reservoir in Central Park. Really? I never knew that Jackie Onassis had her own reservoir. Why would you need one?

I had been planning to visit the museum some time in the near future but having been told, in painful detail, everything about the architecture of the building, its unexpurgated history, contents, floor covering and the names of most of the staff it hardly seemed worth it. As the lecture droned on I stuck a fork in my eye, hoping that it would distract the two vocal bullies from their barrage of data, but to no avail.

'Would you please shut the fuck up before I murder the both of you?' was the phrase hovering on my lips when, mercifully, they decided to leave. 'Cheerio,' I said, with a smile. 'Don't forget to write.'

As we were nearing the last few mouthfuls of our meal, I noticed that there was a plate of boiled eggs next to us that the establishment had provided free of charge which, in my experience, was a rather unusual practice. A plate of nuts, crisps, olives: fine. But boiled eggs? The Chinese lady next to Deb was getting stuck into these faster than Paul Newman in Cool Hand Luke but, mystifyingly, only ate the white albumen whilst leaving the yokes on the side of the plate. Not only was this extremely weird but the place now stank. I could have farted with alacrity throughout my entire meal and escaped scot-free.

With bellies stocked we met Amy and Ryan at *Zinc*. It was a basement jazz club, a bit warren-like, festooned with long scarlet drapes; appealingly bohemian, with much darkness and intrigue. Amy was very New York; loud and feisty, but underneath she was a softie. We all got on famously. The

Brazilian band were excellent and I was surrounded by laid-back, shaggy-haired jazz types who all gave off the impression that if they were told the world was going to end in ten minutes they wouldn't have given a shiny shit. At that moment, I had to admit, the environment was having the same effect on me. I felt my pulse at last beginning to slow in this bustling metropolis.

~~

It was noon before we stirred from our bed having not climbed into it until three thirty this morning. Today we were going to visit Ground Zero. I felt I must attend the site where close to three thousand people perished. I knew two of the moneybrokers, out of the many, who died that day. I was not looking forward to it.

We entered the subway at 51st and Lex on our journey to Wall Street (downtown). The stout, ruddy-faced woman, shoehorned behind the ticket counter, was eating chips from a polystyrene carton as she served me. I asked her three times which train would take me to my desired destination. The effort was nearly too much to bear as she eventually told me to take train six, whilst kindly showing me the mushy-chip contents of her slack mouth.

Nice to see that her employers ran a strict code of behaviour with their staff. As we turned to go, I asked her how the Swiss finishing-school course was going, but she merely wiped her mouth on her sleeve and turned to the next customer.

It was standing room only on the packed train. But here's an odd thing. The guy next to me, on noticing my *are we going in the right direction* look, asked me my destination, then told me to change at the first stop (42nd) and cross to the opposite platform for the number five train. What a helpful chap. If I was standing on a London train looking confused, it would either not be noticed or people would bury their heads swiftly in their own or someone else's newspaper.

This place, I've decided is full of anomalies. One minute I am despairing at the lack of etiquette, general manners and the wealth of ignorance around me, the next I'm being surprised by the warmth, generosity and friendliness of the people. Predictable it wasn't.

When Deb and I reached our new platform I noticed, directly opposite, the sign to Flatbush. Nothing that a quick back-combing and a pair of baggy knickers wouldn't put right, I decided quickly. As I continued to scan my surroundings I registered that the subway was surprisingly clean and graffiti-free – shame about the employees. If it wasn't for that kind gentleman, I could still be rattling around in this city's subterranean maze of tunnels as I write.

We arrived at Wall Street station and were immediately confronted with stalls selling cheap looking disaster booklets of the World Trade Tragedy. Deb turned to me. 'Honestly, I find that so insensitive; making money out of others' misery.'

'Yes, but people have been coining it out of wars and disasters, some way or other, since time began,' I replied, with a sigh.

It goes without saying we didn't buy a booklet.

The reason I am digressing, of course, is that I'm not looking forward to reliving the next part of my experience.

So this was Wall Street. The financial district was so named in the sixteen hundreds, due to an earthen wall that was built to keep out the British. Did nobody like us? In these early days local merchants and traders would gather to sell shares and bonds. It was also a market place where owners could hire out their slaves by the day or week.

In the eighteenth century the area became a residential street. Eventually, due to the economic success of the nearby port, the ground floors of homes were converted into businesses. Then, in the 1830s, the houses were replaced by banks. It was soon realised that due to the lack of space, the only way the financial centre could grow was upwards. And boy, did it!

The evidence of that held us in its towering shadow as we stood gawping up at the freakishly tall offices. I felt like a Lilliputian in the house of Gulliver. Skyscrapers jostled for space on every street. The powerful and claustrophobic personality of the quarter was overwhelming, but, as we turned a corner, we were met by the most remarkable sight – a large expanse of blue sky – an enormous gap that should not be there in an otherwise concrete jungle. The desolate area was Ground Zero.

The temperature had dropped to a very chilly 38°F despite an unobstructed afternoon sun, but suddenly, oblivious to the weather conditions, I was rendered inwardly numb by the forlorn bomb-site of jagged concrete and vast, eerie emptiness. A mesh fence had been erected around the graveyard of innocent souls. On it was a hoarding that narrated in sensitive and non-jingoistic yet defiant terms the events of 11th September 2001.

I was actually sitting at home in front of my television, in stunned silence, watching the horror of it all as it happened. My emotions were a jumble of disbelief, outrage and suffocating despair. I had friends in that building. Now, as I stood on the site where it all happened, I saw the haunted faces at the windows, the frantic human beings trapped in their mid-air offices that, minutes before, were havens of security, hard work and camaraderie – all waiting for certain death. I looked up to see those desperate victims hurling themselves out of their office windows, ninety plus floors up, to escape the intense, scorching heat.

I was overcome with a deep sense of humility. I found myself wiping tears from my eyes that came as a hopeless offering for their cruel and painful deaths. After a while, I tried to put aside as much of the pity I felt as possible and, instead, tried to focus my mind on the human bravery and the bonding instinct of survival when our very being is threatened in such dramatic fashion.

Fifteen minutes had passed and I had not spoken a word to Deborah. She had been making comments and observations during that time but the power of speech had deserted me. It was as if I was trying to listen to the whisperings of the thousands of restless spirits surrounding me.

When I turned away I suddenly felt the cold. I left the site with a jumble of mixed emotions. Our bodies now needed the kind of strength that comes with serious sustenance. We soon found a cafeteria and warmed our bones on two very large cups of tea, which is still regarded as an odd alternative to coffee in this country, and the fattest hamburger on the menu. Replete and refreshed we made our way through the still badly scarred buildings that surrounded the disaster and across to the Hudson River. There to meet us was the indomitable sight of an 1886 gift from the French – the Statue of Liberty.

I was surprised with the effect it had on us two UK citizens. It was strangely reassuring. With our emotions in a very unstable place, this proud symbol of welcome to immigrants seemed, suddenly, to represent the whole of the free world.

As a small aside, lest I get too maudlin here, despite being terribly impressed with the generosity of the Gallic nation towards the US, the question balanced on the very tips of my lips was, 'What have they ever given us, their close neighbours, who fought for their freedom in two world wars?'

As if to tell us it was time to leave, a spiteful wind whipped off the Atlantic Ocean with the apparent intention of taking our noses clean off our faces. We moved sharply inland again and made our way back uptown. What I wasn't expecting, but what our heavy hearts needed, was our sudden arrival at Canal Street – China Town.

Still new to this city, I was amazed to emerge from a deserted street, turn a corner and join a pavement of five-deep, bustling shoppers. I had to blink more than once to take in the sight that appeared, like magic, before our eyes: a market place with a thousand open-fronted shops, which spilt and tumbled along an extensive road and off into the windy distance. To say we were taken aback, well, actually, would be spot-on. This place was nothing like the rest of Manhattan and the suddenness of its appearance excited our senses to the point of putting silly smiles on our faces.

The Chinese proprietors all stood outside their shops with their nothing's-too-much grins and walk-this-way bows. Each store was packed to the gills with cheap jewellery, T-shirts, watches and an enormous collection of bric-a-brac that catered for the memento-seeking tourist trade.

I bought five T-shirts for ten dollars and a hooded New York sweatshirt for twenty dollars. At $1.82 to the pound, that's close to robbery. Deb bought a "genuine" diamond ring for eleven bucks and a knitted black filigree top from an "authentic Chinese clothes boutique", which dripped with silk kimonos in eye-popping Caribbean blues, sunset yellows and lipstick reds.

Our walk home then took us through Little Italy which appeared to be one main street, perhaps four hundred yards long, with the best part of fifty Italian restaurants evenly balanced on both sides of the road. Spoilt for choice, was my immediate reaction to this plethora of Latin pasta palaces.

How could you possibly choose in which establishment to fill your face? More to the point, how could you, as one of the owners, attempt to serve different and original Italian fare from the other forty-nine next door? But they were all open for business, so what do I know? Maybe they were all owned by one large family and shared the profits.

When we arrived back at our apartment, I was, without equivocation, absolutely knackered. I have walked more in the past two weeks than in the two preceding years. I wrenched off my smouldering shoes and as steam filled the room I noticed that my feet were hanging off my ankles like two lumps of raw braising steak. Well, in truth, they ached quite a bit!

We finished the evening slumped in front of the television watching Anne Robinson take the rise, mercilessly, out of a team of African American rappers on The Weakest Link. They were, to a man, woeful in the general knowledge department, which didn't come as a great surprise, but then again I can't rap, so I'll rein in my criticism a tad. Interestingly, despite her initial disdain, little Annie seemed to revel in being surrounded by a dusky herd of muscle-bound hunks. Her roused hormones were spilling out all over the place, making her red hair glow as if it were radioactive.

~~

It was Monday morning and the horns from the unrelenting cavalcade of vehicles coursing down 2nd Avenue reminded me it was business as usual in the big city. I zipped across the road to buy the Sunday Mail (the English papers are one day behind here) at the give-away price of eight dollars. That's nearly four quid and it doesn't even come with the usual ten quires of sundry reading material – no magazines, no free CD's. Someone was making a pretty penny from my quotidian desire to keep in touch with the old country.

We had decided over the weekend that despite our noisy pipes we were fortunate to find such a comfortable apartment and that trying to find another would be far too much hassle. So, I rang Furnished Quarters, our New York lessor, to increase our stay until the fourteenth of May. I wanted to negotiate the same rate of ninety-five dollars per night for the remaining weeks, but could I get to speak to anyone more senior than a recorded answer-phone message? I sent an email and receive nothing by way of a reply.

I am willing to admit that emails have their uses and some advantages over the telephone but, increasingly, I've found that this form of communication is being used as a convenient tool to avoid verbal confrontation. It's so much harder to persuade, be angry, humorous or tickle an ego with someone via the written word.

As emailers, we are stripped of the appliance of inflection; phrase emphasis; pregnant pauses; sighs; harrumphs and, the most precious of all, timing, that all of us employ when dealing with pleasant types and awkward sods alike on the phone.

I fear face-to-face communication will one day be defunct or a novelty at best. You have only to look at a group of youngsters when they are together. There is minimum, if any, conversation amongst them. They all sit around texting other people that are not in their group. It's unhealthy – it's a disease for Christ's sake!

Later, Deb arrived home looking like Rudolph the red-nosed technical analysis sales person. The snowflakes were scampering down again and as quickly as the temperature had ascended toward dizzying spring heights ten days ago, it had dived back down to a bone-shivering thirty-three degrees.

Despite the fierce conditions we still headed off to the gymnasium. Monday night was a bad night to go; there was sweat everywhere. The place was stuffed with people who had pigged out all weekend on Manhattan's lavish portions of restaurant grub and those who had enjoyed the attractions of the myriad of bars that pebble-dashed this merrymaking city.

A filtered version of rich sauces and alcohol seeped from pores, clogging the air, covering the state-of-the-art exercise machines and misting up the long row of picture windows. We added to this, of course, during an hour of purgatory, soaking our recently bought New York T-shirts. Despite this painful ritual we always felt righteous and glowing with health afterwards.

We now both had combination padlocks for our lockers, but to remember how many rotations right and left to arrive at my magic escape number was proving tricky. The first time I used the vicious little sod it took a full five minutes to access my imprisoned clothes. Tonight, as I arrived at my locker tired and soaked in perspiration, I sat and peeled off my kit, which had transformed itself into a second skin. I stood up, recognised my padlock and commenced the safe-cracking routine for a good three or four minutes without success.

'Sod this,' I whispered to myself, 'ridiculous piece of cheap machinery.' I sat down again, in the nude, feeling very weary and very stupid. Elbows on knees, I put my head in my hands, bereft. 'Right,' I said to my feet, 'I can do this. I've got three GCE's and a fifty-yard swimming certificate back home in London. I'm not stupid.'

I took a deep breath and stood up again. As I looked toward the offending item I noticed an identical padlock two lockers along displaying a number, I now remember, to be mine and realised I'd been trying to open someone else's padlock.

'You prize plonker!' I said out loud, and three Americans looked at me with furrowed brows. I smiled, sheepishly. They had obviously never heard of the splendid word "plonker" – or seen one before.

After three aborted attempts I opened my own padlock, put my wet gear in the locker, relocked it and wandered off to have a hot, welcome shower. When I returned, there was a guy opening the padlock that I had, mistakenly, just been trying to open. He was a six feet four Sherman tank. He turned to me and said in a low voice Barry White would've struggled to reach, 'Hi, how ya doin?'

A darned sight better than if you'd caught me trying to break into your locker five minutes ago, I thought.

'Good, and you?' I replied. I dressed with reckless haste and left the changing room glad to be in one piece and expecting to meet a restless Deb. She was nowhere to be seen, so I took a seat outside the ladies changing room and waited. And waited. Twenty minutes passed and I was beginning to worry that she had had a heart attack or some other serious infirmity, when she appeared with a look on her face that portrayed extreme pissed-offedness.

I was about to say, 'Where have you been?' when she held a finger up to her lips. I understood and didn't speak. As soon as we hit the street all was revealed. '

I couldn't unlock my stupid padlock at all,' she explained. 'It wasn't just me, the entire population of the ladies dressing room had a go and all of them failed.'

She went on to say that a brute of a lady supervisor produced an enormous pair of steel cutters (obviously this problem occurs on a regular basis) and, with honed biceps and a theatrical swish, snapped off the lock.

After I added my near-death experience with the Incredible Hulk to my irritated wife's story the air of frustration began to clear and we giggled our way home.

Isn't giggling wonderful! Laughing is great but uncontrolled giggling is just the best.

But seriously, how difficult must it be to devise a combination padlock that actually works? Freddie (fingers) Flaherty, renowned safe-cracker and good egg (to his mum) would, I'm certain, have been totally foxed by these impenetrable components. We decided, as we lay in bed that night, that trusty old-fashioned locks with keys would be the way forward.

~~

We were woken up at five thirty a.m. again by our bloody radiator pipes. I still have had no email back from Brooke, the customer relations officer, in response to my desire to increase our stay and decrease the noisy central heating system. I've got a great idea; I'll send another email, in verse this time, to the tune of Danny Boy. As practically every American claims to be of Irish descent maybe this will rouse someone in the office to offer a reply.

My email went as follows:

Dear Brooke,
Oh, I'm annoyed, the pipes are quite appalling
At sunrise when, they clang and bang inside
To be awoke, each day this way is galling
The noise must go. No more can we abide

So come ye back, the plumbers haven't bled you know
Until the rackets hushed and water flows
And I'll be here, my sunshine, in the shadows
Cos I'm annoyed, I'm so annoyed and full of woe
Regards, Chris.

One hour later, to my surprise I received this reply:

So you're annoyed. The plumber will be calling
At nine a.m. we'll have a man on site
I'll come myself, if it will stop you bawling
You're full of air. My job's to put it right
So we'll come back with plumbers on this very day
And you must trust, we'll take the noise away
And you won't hear, a peep when you are fast asleep
Sincere regrets, hope you are well, have a nice day.
Best, Brooke.

See! All it needed was a dash of original thought and nice to see that the Sceptics have got a sense of humour after all. Good, that's sorted. I was so pleased I thought I'd have a shower to celebrate this breakthrough.

The trouble with this, I remembered as I climbed into the bath, was the abundance of shower curtains. There were three of them draped around me. Taking a shower was like being wrapped in Clingfilm as the vortex, created by the power shower, added to the static electricity from my body, drawing all three plastic layers to my nakedness whichever way I turned.

I stumbled blindly around, feeling like a cross between a freshly wrapped chicken and a vacuum-packed fish, trying to peel off the cold, flimsy, Bostik-like curtains from my face, buttocks and inner thighs. It was like trying to bathe in fly-paper. There was more soap on the bloody curtains than there was on me. After five minutes, I stepped, unclean and dizzy, from the bath to marvel at how refreshed the shower curtains looked.

I don't know. We can land people on the bloody moon but elementary things like padlocks and showers, that should operate seamlessly, still appear to have escaped our powers of attainment. With a small amount of venom, I unhooked the widest plastic leech, tucked it away at the bottom of a wardrobe and stepped back into the bath. Now, each one that hung either side of me stayed where it should, allowing me to enjoy an unmolested shower. How easy was that?

Richard, one of Deb's directors from London, arrived here last night and went into the office today. I am meeting him with Deb tonight at a restaurant on 2nd and 65th. When Deb arrived home, she freshened up in our new non-stick shower, changed into something lovely and we were ready to go. Annoyingly, my chest was wheezing like an old squeeze-box so we decided not to walk the short but freezing distance to the restaurant. We hopped into a taxi for the short ride uptown.

The meal with Richard was both enjoyable and stimulating. Deb offloaded where she thought the New York office could improve. This, from what I understood, appeared to be down to one director who, somewhere along the line, had been mistaken for someone who actually *gave* a shit about the staff, the company's strategy and a thing called success.

Richard took it all on board, looking somewhat embarrassed, and thanked Deb for her polite but candid appraisal. I looked into his eyes and realised, immediately, that nothing was going to change here. It takes an awful lot for a director to sack another and dear Richard was far too nice a chap to swing the corporate axe.

Our deep and meaningful discussion on the future of the company had gone on much longer than anticipated. I looked up to see that we were the last three in the place. Most of the staff had fallen asleep on the floor around our table or buggered off home. Even the cleaners had wiped, scrubbed, mopped and departed. We took the hint to go when the little Italian manager offered us the keys to lock up.

~~

This time it was a coughing fit that woke me up from a restless sleep. My chest was so tight my nipples were beginning to meet in the middle. That's it! I've had enough. The mild cold that I shipped over from my homeland obviously did not like its new surroundings one bit and had morphed into a nasty infection. If I was to be the intrepid explorer on the quest to witness Manhattan's public face and discover her historical underbelly I had to be fit or, at least, not a hacking wreck. Time for the medicine man.

I called Deb who got the number of Amy's family doctor. I rang and was impressed with the offer of an appointment at four p.m. that afternoon. I arrived in a taxi at 74th Street with Deb, who insisted on accompanying me, bless her, and entered the lobby of the very smart building where the doctor made a fortune.

The security man sitting behind the desk was shelling and eating nuts of a kind I've never seen before. He took a cursory glance at us, pulled a rogue piece of shell from his mouth, flicked it into a nearby bin and returned to the more important job in hand. Well, it was nice to know we were in a safely guarded building.

My heart leapt when I saw that the elevator was of the twenty-first century. We took it to the fifth floor and walked out into a lush reception area that made Donald Trump's boardroom look like Del Trotter's front room. I introduced myself to the immaculate and make-up-laden receptionist. She smiled a perfect, sparkling smile and gave me a handful of forms to fill in whilst directing me and Deb to a plush looking seat. I gave the myriad of questions a brief scan. It appeared to want my entire medical history. They ranged from: was I breast fed or bottle fed through to my hopes, dreams and secret desires.

'Excuse me. I have just got a nasty cough and want a few pills,' I said to five layers of face powder. 'I don't think I need...'

'Everyone must complete the medical record, Mr erm...,' she fired back, looking for my name and with a haughty comportment. In a blink, she had switched from pretty secretary to aggressive matriarch. I was expecting her to follow it up with, 'and you can't go out to play unless you've got your vest on.' I looked at Deb, threw my eyes around my sockets, frowned and sat back down.

I waded through questions like: if, when and what did your parents die of: your sibling's health: how often do you take a dump (honestly): when did you give up smoking: are you ashamed about the size of your penis: do you like your eggs over-easy or sunnyside up: do you wear a rubber glove when you masturbate: are you attracted to vicars. The list went on.

Exhausted and feeling a lot worse than when I arrived, I was eventually shown into a tiny room and asked to wait. I waited for a good five minutes. No one appeared. Surely, if the doctor was not ready to see me, wouldn't it have been better to relax in the luxurious waiting area with my loving and sympathetic wife, rather than on my own in a small, medical version of a shoebox? Ironically, the one question that they failed to put on the list was: are you claustrophobic? Luckily, I was not.

Just as I was going to return to the unbridled opulence next door, a young, slim, attractive female doctor squeezed into my closet with me and proceeded to ask me many of the questions that I had just painstakingly answered on all the bloody forms. She then instructed me to pull up the upper part of my clothing to expose my chest. 'I will if you will,' I wanted to say but simply complied with her wish.

With a cold stethoscope, she proceeded to listen to my heart, lungs and anything else that might possibly be making a rattling noise in my upper torso. 'Everything seems to be fine Mr O'Sullivan,' she concluded.

'It's Sullivan. No O. And it might seem fine from where you're sitting but I feel like shit,' I said, as politely as possible.

She offered a gentle smile, ignored my whinging and wrote me out a prescription for strong cough mixture.

She then added that I should book up to see a dermatologist when I returned to England because she had noticed two tiny moles on my back. When I asked her if they looked dodgy she said, 'No, they look perfectly OK.' I wondered why then she mentioned it in the first place.

All that malarkey plus a bill for thirty dollars and a bottle of linctus, which I could have got from the chemist around the corner. On top of that she had decided to put the wind up me by drawing my attention to two little dots on my skin that were perfectly healthy and probably added to the overall character of my body.

Feeling more certain of my longevity and a bit of a fraud, I insisted we walked back to our apartment, stopping off at a Douane Reed chemist. A chemist was known over here, of course, by the subtle and attractive title of *drug store*. My prescription was taken by the pharmacist who told me to wait until my name was called out. There were four other people in front of me.

Twenty-five minutes later, there were six of us standing around, waiting. I was coughing, getting short of patience, but at least I was next on the list to receive my medicine. Then the pharmacist appeared and shouted out, 'Mr Christopher.' *Well, that's not fair*, I thought, I was supposed to be next. I looked around, in an accusing manner, at which of the other maladied individuals had snuck in front of me. No-one came forward.

'Mr Christopher,' she shouted again. Then I realised she was looking across at me as though I was stupid. 'Sullivan Christopher. Hello? That's you, isn't it?' she announced, pointing in my direction and waving my package in front of her face. Now *everybody* in the shop was looking at me as if I was stupid.

'It's Mr Sullivan, actually. Christopher Sullivan,' I replied disdainfully. 'The Christian name tends to take precedence in civilised countries. Anyway, who's called Sullivan as a first name?' I released in a hack, with no small amount of venom and mucus, as I snatched my cough mixture and departed the store. The attractive but brainless doctor's receptionist had obviously copied my name back to front from the form. Honestly, it's not that difficult, is it?

Realising that I was probably going to make it to the end the week, I experienced a sudden adrenalin rush and decided to take Deb into PJ Clarke's for a few libations by way of celebration. We found two seats at the bar just as it began to fill up. Doug, the head barman, who looked like Pierce Brosnan but without the looks, is as sharp as a pin. He remembers everyone's drinks and is on hand to replenish your glass at the sign of an eyebrow twitch – a true professional, especially when he gets us a drink on the house.

When we arrived home I noticed that I was covered in an off-white liquid that had leaked from a bottle of indigestion mixture that was also in the chemist's bag. I now resembled a very bad trainee painter and decorator. What a day. We finally collapsed into our bed just after ten p.m.

'Goodnight, Sullivan,' Deb whispered softly.

'Don't you bloody start!' I rasped.

Chapter Eight

I woke to the sound of silence. No pipes. No cough. I was feeling better already as I trudged off to a hardware store to purchase a stiff brush with which to clean the alkaline mess from my suede jacket, blue cords and suede shoes. I had some success but the cords, by virtue of the ribbed material were being awkward. They would have to go to the dry cleaners.

I stood at my window gazing out at this hundred-mile-an-hour capital, watching the young, expressionless, Filipino delivery men on their bicycles dodging in and out of the constant river of yellow taxis whilst totally ignoring every set of traffic lights. It was a bustling and energetic place out there but I was looking forward to a quiet night in tonight after pushing the boat out over the past week. Just then, Deb rang.

'Don't forget, Chris, we're out on the town this evening with the whole office. It's Richard's last day in New York,' she informed me, enthusiastically.

'Oh! OK. Great!' I lied through my teeth. I arranged to go to her office for the first time since our arrival. 'Yep. Five thirty, I'll be there.' As I put the phone down I wondered where I could buy a new liver in this town.

At the appropriate time I changed into my suit, tie and shiny shoes, checked my make-up, then wandered across and up to 42nd and 5th and past Grand Central station. I had fifteen minutes to spare so I stopped, looked and entered. Wow! What

111

a building. The fascia alone was worth the visit: immaculately scrubbed sandstone-coloured walls, punctured by three massive arched windows, swathed with proud vertical pillars were presided over by solemn looking sculptures of Minerva, Hercules and Mercury. This was more palatial palace than train station.

⊥ I was terribly impressed by this attractive, commanding structure. Rebuilt as Grand Central Terminal (1903-1913), it was the largest train station in the world by virtue of its number of platforms, which were forty-four. It was also ranked number six in the world's most visited attraction. A train station, can you believe?

When I entered the concourse the reason for its popularity immediately became apparent. The inside space was cavernous, the decor majestic. In the centre was a four-faced clock that stood atop the information booth. Each face was lovingly created from opal. Sotheby's had estimated the value to be between ten and twenty million dollars. Blimey! You could cure something nasty with that type of swag.

If you think that's astronomical, you should have seen the ceiling. It was, literally, astronomical. The elaborately decorated domed canopy was of the night sky and its constellations. Apparently, so the story goes, the sky is backwards and the stars are slightly misplaced, but who cares; despite the colourful spectacle giving me a stiff neck, it blew me away. ⊁

The sturdily built terminal backed on to the MetLife building. This brute of a construction, when it was completed in 1963, was the largest commercial office space in the world and was originally the Pan Am building, the headquarters of

Pan American World Airways. Initially, it faced huge unpopularity due to its "ugly" bulk but, whilst I agree that it is not the prettiest edifice around, it possessed an emboldening power somehow and with Park Avenue coming out of its mouth like an enormous welcoming tongue it got an awesome tick from me.

The Metropolitan Life Insurance Company bought the building in 1981. By 1991 the struggling Pan Am company had moved out and, shortly after, folded. A year later, their fifteen foot tall sign was removed from the top of the two hundred and forty-six-metre-high building (that's roughly two and a half soccer pitches – rather you than me) and replaced with the present one.

Originally, the building had a helipad providing a service to Pan Am's terminal at John F. Kennedy International Airport, a mere eight minute flight. But, on May 16, 1977, about one minute after a Sikorsky S-61L landed and its twenty passengers disembarked, the right front landing gear collapsed, causing the aircraft to topple onto its side with the rotors still turning. One of the five, twenty-foot blades broke off and flew into the crowd of passengers waiting to board.

Three men, including film director Michael Findlay, were killed instantly and another man died later in a hospital. The blade then toppled over the side of the building and killed a pedestrian on the corner of Madison Avenue and 43rd Street. Two other people were seriously injured. Not surprisingly, it was the last time the helipad was used.

I've heard of many unfortunate deaths in my time, but to be diced by a runaway helicopter blade must rate very highly on the 'Fuck me, how unlucky can you be' scale; to be

113

squashed by one falling from a roof, well, if it's not your day it's not your day.

Park Avenue is probably my favourite New York thoroughfare and home to some of the most expensive real estate in the USA. It is pleasingly wide, two-way, tree-lined and the most elegant. It has a central reservation and in spring is filled with rows of multi-coloured begonias, a tradition started in 1945 as a memorial to soldiers killed in action. In December, cold weather plants and Christmas trees are placed in the flower border.

When I finally arrived at the building where Deb was temporarily employed, the brute of a security man bent me over his desk, made me spread my legs, whipped down my strides and inserted a Marigold gloved-hand up my rectum. Well, with a stare that hovered somewhere between aggression and lust that's what he looked like he wanted to do. After submitting to a brief body search and promising not to blow up the building, I was allowed to take the lift up to the 52nd floor.

The office in which Deb worked was small and, frankly, a disaster. Haphazard piles of paperwork and heavy files littered every surface. I chicaned my way around cluttered desks, set at odd angles, shimmied past filing cabinets with half-open drawers, stubbed a toe on a cunningly placed metal box, and excused myself through various coffee-drinking employees, who were standing around having a chat, to reach the window where Deb sat.

If she had told me this place had been broken into, burgled and turned over the previous night by some drugged-up, destructive maniac I would have believed her. It was a bloody mess. Then I looked out of the windows, which covered three sides of the office and the surrounding disarray melted away. The views, presented in a steely cobalt sky, were breathtaking. Who needs the Empire State Building when you can sit at a desk, pretend to do a bit of work, have the same panorama, not freeze your balls off and get paid for it?

From the boardroom, which was the only tidy office, I could see the Hudson River and New Jersey to my right and the East River and Queens to my left – the Empire State Building was directly in front of me. Deb was here to galvanise this loss-making branch of her company into one that made a profit. I was tempted to tell her to forget technical analysis, just hire the rooms out by the hour to tourists. You'd make a fortune.

It was 5.35 p.m., the sky was still skin-tinglingly clear and New York was spread at my feet in order to thrill and enchant me. During the next forty minutes, whilst waiting for Deb to finish work, (the only one who *was* working) my vista had gone through a mesmerising change. As the eggshell backdrop slid to a lilac dusk, my view began to take on different dimensions; ten minutes later, it had faded to a deep violet glow, showing me yet another face as the shadows and streetlights transmogrified the shape and texture of this great city.

New York had suddenly been switched on. The skyline now bore a totally different perspective with a million office lights defining the slopes and dimensions of the buildings. The continuous lines of receding red tail lights and oncoming platinum headlights from the never-ending stream of cars, made the roads appear like ever-moving neon signs.

When, eventually, we left the office en masse, some bright spark had decided we all retire to a pub with blaring music. The result was that we had to scream our introductions to each other and continue to converse at perforated eardrum level. It put me in mind of when I was eighteen and trying to chat up girls at cattle market discos that were belting out pop songs at full tilt. Definitely not my best memory.

Mandy was eighteen, Filipino and delightful. Nick was Chinese (now there's a good old Chinese name for you) and didn't stop smiling. Maybe it was because he knew his countrymen would take over the world one day soon; he appeared very amiable.

Next to arrive was Jim, who, would you believe, was also Chinese and he smiled even more than Nick. Then there was Dennis. Mmm! He was dressed in the clothes he obviously slept in. He was an analyst – and it showed, badly. Surely, life's too short to analyse anything – in my experience, you only end up at the point from which you started – most things are best left untouched.

I discovered, during a migraine-inducing conversation with him, that he was married to a Japanese lady and was trying to learn Japanese.

'Have you ever tried to learn Japanese?' he asked, with a dismissive sneer.

'Now, let me think. Erm... probably not.'

He nodded, content with my answer. I very quickly picked up on the fact that this man was decidedly strange. He had this unsettling habit of looking beyond my left ear when in conversation. Twice I looked behind me to see what was of such interest: there was nothing but a bare wall. The kindest thing I can say about Dennis was that he didn't fit into society terribly well.

In fact, just as I was on the point of strangling him with his green and brown striped, beer-stained tie, his exceptionally plain wife arrived wearing glasses the depth of which I'd never seen before. As he turned to buy her a drink, I effected my escape. I very soon found myself in a corner with Richard, where I told him which of his staff I liked, where I thought his company was going wrong and that he was too nice a guy to be a director.

Alcohol can be a dangerous thing but, remarkably, he still appeared to enjoy my company and didn't sack Deb on the spot.

~~

I had been living in New York for close to a month and was getting used to being woken up in the early hours by my beloved tympanic radiators, a never ending procession of booming police sirens and multi-klaxoned, disco-lit fire department trucks that sounded like an amplified herd of constipated cows. However, it was not the silence that I missed, particularly; it was the beautiful Surrey dawn chorus.

To be fair, if I listened carefully, in between the mayhem of man-made Manhattan medleys, I could pick out the occasional sparrow's chirrup or the gurgling coo from a solitary pigeon. But the reassuring symphonies of the blackbird, multi-talented song thrush, chaffinch, robin and blue tit had been snatched from my early morning programme.

We don't realise how much we miss nature's small pleasures until they are taken away from us, do we.

Talking about small pleasures, I managed to buy a packet of cornflakes from the Food Emporium the other day just when I was on the cusp of giving up finding any cereal that I was familiar with. I grew up eating bowls of Kellogg's Cornflakes, and not solely for breakfast, always assuming it was traditional UK conceived sustenance. I was surprised and, frankly, hurt when I discovered in my late twenties, that all my watery-eyed, nationalistic cornflake-wrapped memories were not, in fact, of English origin.

It was Dr John Harvey Kellogg, superintendant of the Battle Creek Sanatorium, Michigan, who created a similar type of recipe as part of a strict vegetarian diet for his patients. The institution's regimen also included no alcohol, tobacco or caffeine. That hangout must have been a bundle of laughs. Will, his younger brother, further developed the cereal to something akin to today's product and decided to attempt to mass-market the new foodstuff. The rest, of course, is history – as is everything from the past.

~~

I rose at seven a.m. on this eerily quiet Saturday morning – I couldn't sleep for some reason. I sat in pants and T-shirt and wrote Friday's entry in my diary. I then woke Deb with tea and toast at eight. The only decent bread I've found here is called Six Grain. It's thin but tasty. That is, until it is toasted, when the heating process sucks out all its stiff-upper-lipiness, leaving it like a soggy Kleenex. The addition of half a jar of marmalade made some amends.

If it seems to you that I'm always moaning about American food products, let me reassure everyone reading this, in case there's any doubt – I am. The product that masquerades as chocolate, for instance, sold on this small island, comes a very poor second to that of the UK. This opinion, I add quickly, is supported by all the US staff in Deb's New York office. They plead on bended knee and promise to hand over their pension rights and family heirlooms to her if she will bring suitcases packed with English chocolate every time she flies from London on a trip over here. They lust after Cadbury's Fruit and Nut, Kit Kats, Mars Bars, and Curly Wurly's, to mention just a few.

So, why is this? US chocolate is either wan and tasteless or dark and bitter and never scrummy. What is the point, I ask you, of eating something you shouldn't, when it doesn't even taste nice? In my experience, everything I have ever read or been told is bad for you, without exception, either makes you fat, give you spots, piles or a heart attack. To make up for this, we have the '*I shouldn't really's*. These treats always have a wicked, delicious, guilty and self-indulgent pleasure attached to them – you know: smoking a crafty joint, strong coffee, jam doughnuts, suet pudding, six pints of beer, under-age sex with your French Conversation teacher. Not American chocolate. I don't get it.

We are blessed with another, isn't it great to be alive, blue sky over Manhattan. We seized the moment and took a fifteen minute wander up to Central Park. Bathed in sunshine it was a wonderful, heart-warming sight, but our hearts were the only portions of our bodies, in actual fact, that were warm. The North East wind was cutting through the streets from the East River in ice-tipped spears. I was suddenly very grateful that Deb made me put on a ridiculous amount of clothing and a baseball cap.

✦ Central Park is a broad, soft green stripe of celestial bliss running down the back of a frenzied, hard-skinned creature that is Manhattan Island. Within its eight hundred and forty-three acres of land, it has lakes-a-plenty, theatres, ice-rinks, fountains, tennis courts, baseball fields, a zoo and a museum of art and boasts two hundred and seventy different species of birds. It was, to us city bound Brits, an oasis of peace, sanity and relative quiet.

And this is how it all began.

In 1857, a competition was organised for the design of a new park. The remit was to rival the great parks of London and Paris. After much deliberation Frederic Law Olmsted and Calvert Vaux got the nod to convert the vast area of swampland into their vision of loveliness. It took fifteen years and a procession of twenty thousand workers before it was finished. That's some project.

Shamefully, from around 1960 through to 1980 the park went into decline and, sadly, became the home to graffiti, garbage and criminals. It was only when a group of citizens formed the Central Park Conservancy and persuaded the city to fund a fifty million dollar renovation project that the park was cleaned up and restored to its former pomp. Ever since then it has been regarded as a clean and safe (certainly during the daytime) place of leisure. ✦

As we sauntered beneath extravagant brick arches, through bird-thronged forests, around soul-soothing serene lakes it was impossible to believe that we were smack in the middle of a thriving city. One of the architectural highlights was the Bethesda Terrace where we now found ourselves. From our standpoint we overlooked the imposing fountain with its eight foot bronze statue of the Angel of the Waters, the lake and the boathouse. This was a perfect place to have our picture taken and, as luck would have it, a Chinese tourist was within arm's reach. The diminutive gentleman seemed beside himself to be asked to perform this small task.

I handed him our idiot proof camera and with our best smiles we stood posing and waiting; and waiting; and waiting in the blood-chilling arctic conditions. In his unbounded excitement, his first three attempts were unsuccessful as his impatient little fingers pushed and prodded every spot on the device apart from the correct button. His frenzied digits were finding knobs and catches I didn't know existed on the bloody machine. 'Ah! Solly,' he apologised. By this time our frozen smiles had set hard on our frozen faces. At the onset of each failed attempt, he announced in a high-pitched, gleeful voice, 'OK. Leady. One, two, three… smile, preese.'

'For goodness sake! How difficult can it be, you silly little man?' I ached to say. Just as I was about to step forward, grab my camera and thrust him backwards into the icy waters of the fountain he finally located the appropriate plastic pimple and took the picture. He then had the cheek to ask me to return the favour, handing me his expensive Nikon.

'Ten dollars,' I managed to squeeze through blue, frigid lips, holding out an even bluer hand and I think I may have got it had Deb not giggled in embarrassment.

After slapping the circulation back into one another's faces, we continued up through the park to Strawberry Fields. As we paused by the shrine to John Lennon I made a point, on this occasion, to recount only happy memories of this talented man.

Through the park we strolled, soon to be ascending a testing rise where we happened upon Belvedere Castle, the highest point of the park. It was completed in 1872 purely as a viewing pavilion. This rather striking construction was intended to be a Victorian folly with no intended purpose other than to impress its audience whilst taking in the surrounding views. I have to say that it achieved that aim quite splendidly.

We stood, the wintry breeze dancing through our hair, as we gazed down over Turtle Pond, ingeniously named because an extravagant amount of turtles had decided to make it their permanent residence and it was a pond. Our attention was then grabbed by the massive expanse of grass named the Great Lawn (don't ask) that was divided and marked out by half a dozen baseball pitches.

As we stood peering in a haughty manner down on this mollifying panorama a bunch of unruly youths decided to commence *let's see who can be the loudest and most irritating prick* competition. I suppose I must have been a testosterone-filled pain-up-the-backside at times in my youth, but I offered little appreciation as these performing halfwits somewhat spoiled our moment of imagined grandeur and the majesty of the castle.

Our cold and weary limbs then managed to lead us down to the Metropolitan Museum of Art, which was where the outbound portion of our arctic expedition ended. We didn't venture inside as there were at least twenty stalls set up outside that were selling many wonderful and varied paintings, drawings and photos of this vibrant city.

Suffused with this impressive assortment of images we schlepped back homewards through the park until we met Alice in Wonderland with friends, White Rabbit and the Mad Hatter, all cast in a warm shiny bronze. A few paces further on we bumped into a pile of red bricks that sat beneath a green copper roof. This ensemble was entitled Kerb's Memorial Boathouse. It was a welcome discovery as both of our whistles were now in dire need of wetting. So, we stopped for a cuppa and two passionless efforts at cakes that were completely devoid of even a hint of moisture. If it wasn't for the tea we would have still been trying to swallow the dusty contents by nightfall. Mr Kipling these were not.

In front of the boathouse was a sizable, shallow lake that, I discovered, was used in the warmer seasons for model boating. Now, call me an old stick-in-the-mud, but I am in a state of constant bewilderment by adult obsessional fervour for children's pastimes such as flying kites, remote controlled airplanes and model-boat demonstrations. Did you know that the current World Yo-yo champion is in his mid-twenties, for pity's sake? My yo-yo went straight in the bin the day after my first pubic hair popped out of my y-fronts. Have these people never discovered sex, sport, music, beer, crime?

Dry-caked and rosy-leed, we pushed on towards our home – old Central Park leaving us with an agreeable flush.

~~

Although our apartment was a single block away from the East River it was the one direction in which we had not ventured. So, being Sunday, we both decamped silently and eastwards. Whether I had a sixth sense I cannot say, but the result was very disappointing. The area was bleak and windy with rows and rows of characterless apartment blocks that seemed to be in permanent shadow.

What did catch our attention was that each bar we passed was gearing up for St Patrick's Day which was the coming Wednesday. In fact, every single bar in Manhattan, be it Irish or not, was hanging up green sparkly bunting and paper shamrocks with gay abandon.

I was told it would be a night to remember, although I had been warned by some that I may experience some anti-English feeling from the odd over-patriotic quasi-Irishman. I really hoped that would not be the case. I had stood shoulder to shoulder with many Irish friends over the years and joined in on their night of celebration, but a little seed of doubt had been planted.

Chapter Nine

'I don't like Mondays. Tell me why? I don't like Mondays,' I was informed, many years ago by the Boomtown Rats. And, despite the unsatisfactory answer, I have to agree with them. The day started all too familiar. I rang Furnished Quarters to remind them that the pipes were still clanging away but it took me an hour to manage to speak to a living person. He promised immediate action, but I am not expecting it.

Realising I needed to push myself beyond the boundaries of the weekly washing I decided to spend the afternoon checking out the Rockefeller Center. My leisurely stroll took me along 50th for three blocks, where I hung a right into the capacious and well-presented Park Avenue. Here's where I came face to face with the celebrated Waldorf Astoria Hotel. In truth, I find the facade of this building prosaic in the extreme and not a patch on the original.

The first Waldorf Hotel, all thirteen storeys of it, designed by our old friend Henry J Hardenbergh opened in 1893 on the corner of 5th Avenue and 33rd where millionaire developer William Waldorf Astor had his mansion. In 1897 his cousin, John Jacob Astor IV, again with the help of Henry's creative bent, opened the seventeen storey Astoria Hotel on the adjacent site. A corridor was built to connect the two buildings and voila, the Waldorf-Astoria was born. Sadly, JJ Astor died tragically fifteen years later in the pitiless, icy North Atlantic

Ocean when the stricken Titanic disappeared beneath the waves.

The magnificently constructed hotel gained worldwide admiration for its luxury and elegance but by 1920, for reasons I've yet to discover, it was thought to be outdated. The Astor family made the decision to sell the land, the hotel being demolished on the 13th May 1929. The Empire State Building now stands on that very site. The present Waldorf Astoria opened in its current location in October 1931 and was the tallest and largest hotel in the world at that time. Shame about the design though.

Turning left down 50th, I crossed over Maddison Avenue and up to 5th Avenue where I found the Rockefeller Center. The first thing that caught my eye on arrival was the adjacent sunken ice-skating rink, encircled by rows of fluttering flags of the United Nations member countries. A magnificent bronze gilded statue of the Greek Titan Prometheus, who, on first glance, appeared to be sliding down a small mountain into a pool of water with unabashed glee, oversaw this peculiar, rotary form of merriment. The backdrop, with spurting talon-like fountains emerging through dramatic, submerged lighting, made the entire display appear as if it was on fire.

Seeing the citizens of this mad city gliding along the lustrous mercury surface in absent-minded circles without, what appeared to be, a care in the world put a large and soppy smile upon my face. The pink-cheeked, unbridled fun and frolics that played out before me was such a pleasant surprise.

How complicated but wonderfully reassuring is the human species. Envelop us with towering columns of concrete and expansive roads filled with vehicles piloted by intolerant psychopaths and we are serious, hurried, introvert. Yet, if someone plonks a splodge of off-white slippery stuff in the middle of all this chaos and rents out pointy-soled boots that you can't stand up in, we are enticed into dreamland. Souls lost in an existence where nothing matters more in life than managing to stay vertical whilst sliding along in a forward direction; this being, in most cases, with a minimum degree of dignity and in the hope that you will end up where you started from with bones intact and a full complement of fingers.

That's how easy it is to transform sober, business-like adults into squealing childlike buffoons. It was both astonishing and a delight to witness.

A successful man was old JD Rockefeller. Born in Richford, New York in 1839, his parents moved to Cleveland, Ohio when he was fourteen years old. Two years later he began work as a bookkeeper. In 1859, aged twenty, he started up a business with partner Maurice Clark, each putting up two thousand dollars as commission merchants in grain, hay, and meats. In two years they had made a profit of seventeen thousand dollars, not bad for the mid-nineteenth century, and moved into oil refining two years after that, in 1863.

Standard Oil was created in 1870. Rockefeller's wealth soared in the following years, making him the world's richest man and the first American to be worth more than a billion dollars. He retired in 1897, aged fifty-eight, when his son, JD Junior, took over the business.

Junior, admirably, wanted to use this vast fortune to the furtherment of the US. Amongst many other projects, he set up the Rockefeller Institute for medical research (now Rockefeller University) and founded The General Education

Board establishing a raft of high-schools throughout the country. In 1930, he commissioned the country's leading architects to build the Rockefeller Center. The buildings were completed and opened to the public in 1939. It was the first real estate project to include offices, retail, entertainment and restaurants in one integrated development. It was built, initially, to house the up-and-coming radio and TV industry with RCA, RKO and NBC being its primary tenants. The Center is a complex of nineteen commercial buildings set over twenty-two acres between 48th and 51st Streets and 5th and 6th Avenues with an estimated one million visitors a year.

The showpiece is the seventy-floor GE Building (General Electric), which stands at some eight hundred and seventy feet high and looks just like the type of structures I used to erect with my Meccano set as a nine-year-old. In front of this neck-breaking vertical monster stood the dusky, forty-five-foot bronze statue of Atlas, who possessed more tumescent, shiny muscles laminating his body to which any man has a right.

It was the GE Building where, in 1932, the famous black and white photo Lunchtime Atop a Skyscraper was taken. This showed a line of construction workers sitting on a steel beam, without safety harnesses, eating their lunch above a two hundred and sixty-metre drop to the ground below. Apparently, it was a publicity stunt to promote the new construction. I have a copy of that celebrated picture in my home and all I can say is rather them than me.

~~

What a difference a day makes. The gentle, pastel sky had been stolen and smuggled out of the country during the night. In its place the thieves had left a dirty grey ill-fitting blanket that billowed a short distance above the streets. Snow was falling from this oppressive cloak in flakes so large it was as if a billion white tennis balls were tumbling down in slow motion to form a spotless, crisp, deep-pile carpet over the floor of Manhattan.

Whilst we are on the subject, I have always thought it unfathomable why snow-filled clouds are such an unprepossessing, murky grey colour whilst the stuff that tumbles out of them is so graceful and perfectly white? Whatever the reason, the temperature had hurtled rapidly back to freezing and the wind had become impatient and tetchy, barging past people with no thought for their comfort or safety.

This sudden meteorological drag-back had lowered my spirits to a level hovering between advanced frustration and elementary depression, but the need to escape from my apartment every day was fundamental to my mental and physical wellbeing. Wearing my wardrobe with the addition of a baseball cap I released myself out into the elements. The snow was already two inches deep and of the unfeasibly slippy variety. My boots were, disconcertingly, shooting off in all directions on the ends of legs that were flailing around like two strands of spaghetti.

I tried to maintain my composure as I performed a forward version of the moonwalk along previously unremarkable roads that were now transformed into flawless corridors of luminescent silver. It seemed that in whichever direction I plodded, the wind was blowing the snow straight into my eyes, up my nose and across my quick-to-chap lips.

But do you know what? There was something glorious, and I only seem to experience this in foreign lands, about completing my miniature expedition. As I struggled through the streets of New York in hostile conditions I experienced a smug feeling of triumph. I was Amundsen and Mallory heading out into the unknown, through uncharted territory, in life-threatening circumstances. Could I survive the hazardous elements? Could I make the long, merciless yards to the paper shop?

The austere grey of the concrete buildings and pavements were now decked with glistening capes of ermine – the harsh drone of ceaseless traffic soothed and softened by this phenomenon of weather fronts. A thousand dustbin lids, normally leaden, stained, dented, had become flawless ivory-topped mushrooms, standing like squat sentries outside each shop front.

I arrived, victorious, at my destination, bought shares in Associated Newspapers, tucked my Daily Mail under my arm and retired to Lenny's for a pastrami special and latte. It was warm and welcoming. I took a window seat. Here I sat, read, filled my belly and watched the snow-spattered and unsteady citizens of New York paso doble past my cosy viewing post. It was there, at that glass-covered observation point, that I was a fortunate witness to a piece of pure theatre.

A portly, middle-aged gentleman with a very small dog, wrapped tightly in a tartan waistcoat, approached my window in a very gingerly fashion. He was wearing one of those hats that had the long, droopy, furry ear attachments making him look like Deputy Dawg. As he drew level with me he slipped, in spectacular fashion, flipped upwards achieving a perfect horizontal plain and with pike, landed flat on his back in the thick snow.

The dog, spooked by his master's antics ran twice around him in a frenzy, crouched down and, I assumed in a confused and agitated frame of mind, had a quick shit behind his back, the temperature of which caused it to settle quickly below the snow's surface. The man, shaken but seemingly unhurt apart from his ego, and unaware of his pooch's bodily function, put one arm behind him to get up, his hand disappearing straight into the middle of the dog turd.

As I sat transfixed, trying to stifle a guffaw, I was unspeakably impressed when the man's expression and demeanour did not change one iota.

He clambered up onto his feet, brushed himself down with his clean hand and gathered up the nearby lead. He then drew the dog close, whispered a few words in the ear of the confused animal, wiped his hand down the length of its chequered back, gave it a swift kick up the arse and slowly disappeared into the blizzard as if it was an everyday occurrence.

I had often wondered why some big men prefer to have little dogs as pets. It has all become patently clear. If you make a fool of yourself in public, you can take it out on the small creature without fear of it ripping your face off.

~~

Still snowing – but the flakes are now only the size of dimes. Today is 17th March, St Patrick's Day, which is almost as big a deal as Christmas Day in England. As I crossed over 2nd Avenue to get my daily paper, I noticed that everything had been dressed in green. Green flags and bunting joined buildings to lampposts, lampposts to shop blinds.

Everyone appeared to be sporting at least one bright green item of clothing or badge or silly hat or stick-on face transfer. It seems to me that every American I meet over here lays claim to having an Irish connection however tenuous – a distant relative; being able to sing some of the words to Danny Boy; knowing someone who once drank a pint of Guinness. Aware of the Irish contingent in this town, be they real or wannabe's, I knew Paddy's Day would be big. I had no idea how big. The place had gone green barmy.

Saint Patrick (AD 385-461) was the most commonly recognised of the patron saints of Ireland. His day has been observed for over a thousand years, but was only made an official Christian feast day in the early seventeenth century. It commemorates St Patrick and the arrival of Christianity in Ireland as well as celebrating the heritage and culture of the Irish people.

Interestingly, the first parade held to honour St Patrick's Day took place, not in Ireland, but in the USA. On 17th March 1762, Irish soldiers serving in the English military marched through New York City. Along with their music, the parade helped the soldiers reconnect with their Irish roots.

The celebration fell during the Christian season of Lent, but restrictions on eating and drinking alcohol were lifted for the day, which encouraged the holiday's tradition of making merry and providing a great excuse to get rat-arsed.

Last night, Kieran, my friendly Irish barman, gave me two tickets for the Official Reviewing Stand hastily assembled on 64th and 5th. Deb was, of course, working, so, at ten thirty a.m., I made my way up there in the freezing cold and still fairly persistent snow. Here I found half a dozen corpses frozen to the open-air metal seats of a somewhat rickety-looking tiered viewing platform. They were all staring into nothing.

The parade, boasting floats and marching school bands, was supposed to commence at ten a.m. By eleven, the iced cadavers had swelled to around thirty and still the streets were free of any form of entertainment. I heard myself saying 'fuck this for a game of soldiers,' into my frost-encrusted scarf and promptly sloshed my way back to my welcoming apartment. With piping hot cup of tea in hand and digestive biscuit hanging loosely from my mouth I found excellent TV coverage of the parade and saw everything I wanted from the comfort of my large and squeaky mock-leather sofa.

So I can say, only cheating a little bit, that I was there in New York at the St Patrick's Day parade. I witnessed a procession of multi-coloured floats that glided over the snow, followed by nicely chilled but smartly dressed school kids, who sang and played there little hearts out, and I lived to tell the tale.

The night was bedlam. Every bar was filled to bursting with all-day drinkers. We couldn't even get through the door of the first three we tried. Eventually we found a small pub down a skinny alley. Again, the bar was packed tighter than Dolly Parton's brassiere, but we managed to squeeze ourselves in. Smack in the middle of the bar stood a huge, hairy man on the bagpipes accompanied by a small man, with less hair, on the bodhran (hand-held drum), gaily banging out all the old Irish favourites.

Deb and I felt a little bit out of it at first as all in the pub appeared to be as pissed as parrots. But you know what Irish diddly music is like. Before I even had the chance to be served, my feet suddenly gained a mind of their own and started to flap around in a reckless manner to the heady, frantic beat. The involuntary spasms very quickly shot up through my body where I noticed my hands slapping together in front of my face like a mechanical monkey but without the cymbals. My Sullivan ancestry was truly awoken, springing to life in front of my traitorous English eyes.

I swung around to notice that Deb was suffering from the same musical affliction. The atmosphere was so infectious that after a few libations served, alas, in plastic glasses we both began to lend our voices to the Celtic airs and blabber away to the smiling faces around us as though they were our long lost cousins. This last part was impossible not to do on account of everybody being squeezed together like cigarettes in a packet.

The prices of drink had been hiked up for the night and the safe but disagreeable plastic glasses were nowhere near a pint measure. Despite the pub landlord taking outrageous advantage of his customers on their big day of celebration, we had a jolly evening without a hint of aggressive behaviour.

~~

When we had first moved into this apartment, the letting company had only just taken over the building and put it on their books. They had also acquired a few problems along with their 'highly des res in sought after area of Manhattan', as had been highlighted by our niggly complaints. The maintenance that had been carried out over the preceding years was clearly not up to standard.

The one advantage to this was that the management were almost certainly aware of these imperfections, despite their denials. The rent they were charging me gave them away. It was a mere ninety-five dollars per night, which was, as I have found out here, exceptionally low-priced for this type of accommodation and the part of town we were in. The management knew, of course, that as soon as they had addressed the building's problems and stuck an extra TV in each apartment they could charge their tenants a significantly higher rent.

That is why they've just informed me that, as of 1st May, they will be hiking the rent up to one hundred and forty dollars per night. This came as a bit of shock when I realised that we were due to leave on 14th May. I was worried that I would not be able to negotiate a contract till that date without a rise in our rental charge. We were already at the maximum allowance granted by Deb's company so, if I failed, we were in serious trouble. When I realised that we should be paying one thousand three hundred and fifty dollars more per month for our comfortable bolt-hole, those clangy pipes didn't seem so loud any more.

Outside of our bargain-base apartment it was still snowing but in a rather apathetic manner. The wind though still had a nasty bite to it as it rushed up the broad avenues that were the main arteries of Manhattan, and filtered through the multitude of streets – the capillaries connecting the life-flow of this vibrant capital. Each time I wandered around in the shadows of this lofty environment, it was impossible not to feel the awesome power of the institution that was New York. I found it slightly scary and yet protective at the same time, if that makes sense.

As it was Friday and Deb didn't have to work the following day we decided to visit the renowned Asian themed nightspot/restaurant, Tao. Deb had visited this venue a few months ago with some work colleagues and she had not stopped going on about it from the moment our plane had landed at JFK Airport.

When she led me to the small, innocuous front door I was a little disappointed. *What type of dive is this going to be?* tickertaped across my thoughts. But wow, this was the Tardis ten times over with some to spare. The cavernous interior blew me away. I challenge anyone to walk through that door as a new customer and expect anything close to the sight that is set out before them.

The building was designed originally as a 19th century stable for the Vanderbilt family – one of the oldest and most renowned in America – whose success began with the shipping and building empires of Cornelius Vanderbilt. Sometime later the huge edifice became a balconied cinema. It was then transformed into a majestic Asian Temple opening for business under the name of Tao in the autumn of 2000.

The bare brick internal walls were adorned with artefacts from China, Japan and Thailand. These were made all the more dramatic by the discreet, moody wall lighting and six gigantic raffia lanterns that hung menacingly high above our heads. Most of the ceiling was covered by three enormous white sheets. With the aid of enthusiastic air-conditioning fans, they billowed back and forth like the sails of a ship, revealing large Chinese writing beneath. It was quite spectacular.

The imposing focal point was a sixteen-foot-tall Buddha situated at one end that floated above a virtual reflecting pool complete with Japanese carp. The diners were provided with three hundred seats situated on three different levels and served by waiters dressed as houseboys. The place was packed and buzzing. I don't recall ever being so mightily impressed by the interior of a building – and I have poked my head in a few swanky venues, I can tell you.

The continuous booming pulse of the dance music created a kind of hypnotic, jungle fever. It put me in mind of ancient African tribes dancing in a mesmeric trance throughout nights filled with witchcraft and magic spells. What a night. You have to go.

At two thirty a.m., we finally waved the white flag; we left the younger revellers at the still lively nightspot and retired to our kingsize bed.

I woke with a thick head, peeled my tongue off the wall, which had left my mouth in search of water sometime during the night, and drank every ounce of fluid that was in our fridge. It was not the best way to start a weekend. After our fifth cup of tea we decided that maybe we should take in more oxygen with our liquids so we ventured out into a cold but, once again, bright and sunny day. Up to Grand Central Station we ambled and as Deb had not been inside, we slunk in. I know I have covered this earlier but I have to expound on my first description, such is the impression this venue had upon me.

Both the exterior and interior of this building were truly breathtaking. The astrological ceiling, conceived by French artist Paul Cesar Helleu, was cast in a deep turquoise, covering twenty-two thousand square feet and, like a clear night sky, it gave the impression that it was miles above our heads. The entire place was kept spotlessly clean and had the feel and look of a museum rather than a train station.

Biscuit coloured stone arches inscribed with gold letters heralded the many tunnels and walkways that burrowed and weaved through this tribute to architecture. This edifying structure housed restaurants, hotels, offices and an indoor market, which sold fresh produce, meats and confectionary displayed with the precision and care usually afforded to a jeweller's window.

The most revered eaterie, the Oyster Bar, no prizes for guessing, was a seafood restaurant. Visited by the rich and famous, it sat beneath numerous, dramatically lit vaulted arches in an atmosphere that reeked of cool sophistication. It was also renowned for its whispering gallery. Due to an acoustical quirk, it was possible to hear low volume conversations from one corner of the room to the other. It may be a novelty to some but I thought it should have had "Danger!" or "Beware!" written on the entrance door. Imagine a table full of dignitaries discussing state secrets over their hors d'oeuvres, whilst carefully-placed undercover agents are taping every word; or portly red-faced ageing executives trying to talk their nubile secretaries into bed, when half the restaurant are hanging on each cringeworthy chat-up line and giggling into their scallops.

Later that afternoon I took two pairs of my wife's shoes to the cobbler's shop to be soled and heeled. This may sound a little weird but I've always loved the smell of a shoe repairer's. I don't know if it's the leather or the glue; maybe the cobbler himself, but it's a sort of down-to-earth reassuring aroma that belongs, somehow, to the distant past; a time of blacksmiths and horse-drawn carriages, gas lamps and Cliff Richard. Every time I enter one of these little shops, I always expect the cobblers to look like Geppetto, the toy maker in Pinocchio – you know – the little, old bloke with long white hair and a walrus moustache. They never do, of course.

Chapter Ten

This was a bad morning for me. I should have felt privileged to be supported financially for doing nothing in New York, but that was precisely the problem. Yes, I was getting to know this fascinating city but apart from my daily diary I was, in my mind's eye, not doing enough in New York. I was beginning to feel surplus to requirements and it was starting to get to me.

The occasional quandary, the seed of doubt, which undermines every writer who has not been commissioned to produce a piece of work arrives in the form of, 'Am I wasting my time... will anyone ever read this?' And having been the fortunate beneficiary of this semi-vacation, so generously supplied by my wife's bosses, I was feeling somewhat underemployed.

But then, I reasoned, if every aspiring writer gave in to those disruptive whispers the world would have no novelists, journalists and poets whatsoever. So, I thought, sod it! I'm off into the unknown with eyes peeled and pencil in pocket. Racing down the stairs, I skipped past Lionel, pushed through the double doors and turned right.

I thought I'd check out 1st Avenue in more detail. There has to be something of interest up here, I determined, as I wandered at a leisurely pace along the East River in an uptown direction. My first observation was that the fast flowing expanse of grey/brown water was as about as attractive as the

Thames in London. Actually, the East River, in the true sense of the word, is not a river at all because it connects on both ends to the Atlantic Ocean. As a matter of fact, it's a tidal strait, whereas the Hudson River, which trundles down Manhattan's West Side, is your actual pucker river. It starts its journey from Lake Tear, its northern source in The Peaks, moving down south till it meets the ocean.

After walking past an endless procession of large, unprepossessing, grubby buildings, half of which looked abandoned, I found a seat next to the swirling flow. It was smack bang next to the rusting iron monstrosity that was Queensboro Bridge, also known as 59th Street Bridge for obvious reasons. The cantilever construction connects Manhattan to the borough of Queens on Long Island, passing over Roosevelt Island. After many teething problems the bridge opened to the public on 30th March, 1909. The viaduct has two levels catering for vehicles, cycles and pedestrians. It cost in the region of eighteen million dollars and was responsible for the loss of fifty lives.

A sobering thought has just hit me. The more I learn about the building of early twentieth century bridges the more I realise how incredibly hazardous the process was to human life.

'We've got some great news and some not particularly great news,' I can hear Chuck, the recruitment head of the Department of Bridges, announce to an eager assembly of unemployed workers. 'We've got a good five years work for all of you, but, erm, there's a fair chance, well, put it this way, I wouldn't bet on all of you being around to take a stroll with the missus over the finished article. OK? Sign here.'

My second thought, as I sat frostbitten on my bench beneath coat, scarf and gloves was that as soon as the weather lent itself to being a little less unkind I would bring my notebook here and write. I could sit facing the river and scribble at one of the few wide open spaces to be found in this tight-fitting city whilst not having to share my car-fume-flavoured oxygen intake with a cluster of wheezing lungs.

Despite a smart wind skipping over the water and me, I basked in the peaceful luxury of not being bullied by skyscrapers and endless lines of hostile traffic as I watched the broad and wayward *tidal strait* hurry quietly back to its mother, Mrs Atlantic Ocean.

After perhaps twenty minutes, I departed the riverside pew and continued uptown for a few blocks, hung a left and rejoined 1st Avenue. Ah! This part of town was a bit more interesting. Designer clothes shops, tapas bars, Mexican restaurants and a comedy club called Dangerfield's lined the avenue. I was surprised that a distance of a few hundred yards could make such a difference to the ambience of the area.

It was far brighter and livelier than the drab 1st Avenue that cut ingloriously past my apartment block. The people were different; they were more relaxed and appeared less focused on getting to somewhere else.

I scanned the window of Dangerfield's nightclub to see an impressive array of past performers and guests that included Jim Carrey, Jay Leno, Adam Sandler, Michael Douglas, Johnny Carson and many, many more. Rodney Dangerfield, I learned later, was one of America's best loved stand-up comedians who died at the aged eighty-two, on 5th October 2004, five months after we returned home to England.

On her return from work, Deb told me she had just experienced a particularly exacting day. She deserved a treat. So, tonight, we were going posh and bugger the expense. I decided on The View, a revolving rooftop bar and restaurant sitting atop the Marriott Marquis Hotel in Three Times Square. This was the most extravagantly illuminated quadrangle into which I had ever stepped. It was impossible not to be seduced utterly by the massive array of bright lights of every shape, dimension and colour imaginable.

As we entered the ground floor of the hotel, a billion-windowed monstrosity sprouting from a collage of gigantic neon advertising signs, we were approached by a smartly dressed concierge. He directed us to the elevator, which turned out to be a glass capsule. This was launched upwards at an impressive rate inside the core of the building with open views of all the different floors. These rapidly passing tiers were filled with restaurants, gymnasiums and row upon row of bedroom doors. After this, seemingly unattached, vertical flight, we taxied smoothly alongside the 48th floor trying not to look down at the immense distance from whence we had just been propelled.

As we stepped from the elevator, which put me in mind of a tiny bead of sweat clinging precariously to the inside of a giant pint glass, we found ourselves in the bustling restaurant. This was a massive circular platform that revolved slowly around a static central structure. We were surrounded by picture windows affording a three hundred and sixty degree vista of Manhattan at night: a panorama of twinkling lights and shadowy buildings – a rotating goldfish bowl in the stars.

It took just over an hour to complete a full lap in our barely noticeable spinning room. Deb had the seared snapper and I climbed aboard the roast saddle of lamb. Did we feel grand, sipping cocktails and going round in circles in our seductively-lit glass tower? You bet we did.

If you're not scared of heights and see-though lifts that have no visible means of support then this is the place for you. And for those of you with a more cavalier sense of adventure, I would recommend trying the Chelsea Cosmopolitan cocktail. One will make you feel warm and squishy, two could loosen the taciturn tongue of a Trappist monk.

~~

I raised myself from our bed at five thirty a.m. this morning to help my wife pack and prepare for an overnight trip to Toronto. Deb and New Yorker Amy, the youngest member of the sales team, are visiting a Canadian bank in an attempt to secure a lucrative contract for the company. As I've mentioned, Deb was born in Toronto and possesses a Canadian passport even though she's as English as a sack of King Edward spuds. Her British parents met in Toronto, married, had Deb and moved back to England a year later. So, although officially Canadian, she's not.

Later in the morning I received a text stating that she had arrived safely after a short one hour flight. I thought Canada was a longer schlep from New York – just goes to show that I should have paid more attention to Mr Crawshawe in my geography lessons at school.

It's strange how your interests shift as you get older. During my school years I regarded history and geography on a par to brass rubbing and, consequently, have a rather chequered knowledge of these subjects today. But, as the reality dawns that I am now more history than future I seem to be developing a fascination of the whys and whereabouts of the world of which these two subjects seem to know all the secrets.

I stayed in tonight and had beans on toast, but something was missing. It wasn't the tomato sauce – it was the wife. The apartment, unexpectedly, felt strangely empty. Was I lonely? Blimey! This never happens at home when Deb is away on an overseas trip. It must be because I'm in a foreign land, I suppose.

Travelling is great for the soul. It's an education, a release, a chance to breathe in unfamiliar air, to witness different cultures of people that, fundamentally, have the same pleasures and problems as you. But to do it on your own for weeks, months, friendless days, solitary nights in cheerless hotel rooms? Give me a partner every time.

Still, I'm a big boy, I told myself, so I quickly rallied. As if to come to my rescue, I found an obscure TV channel showing a re-run of a 1999 football match between Manchester United and Southampton. David Beckham looked about twelve years old.

Thinking about it, he still looks about twelve years old, but the programme filled me to the brim with Englishness, dragging me closer to home in those ninety rapturous minutes. I topped the evening off with a cup of Typhoo tea and a couple of ginger snaps. They prefer to call them *snaps* to our *nuts*

145

(there's a phrase I doubt you'll hear again in your lifetime). I then retired to my empty bed and everything was back to normal apart from the cold space next to me.

~~

On my first day alone in this city I decided, after all, to visit the Guggenheim museum on the East Upper Side, situated between Central Park and the East River – which happens to be a museum hotspot. Despite those two buffoons plying me with a forty minute running commentary on the place, I thought I should give it a go.

The eye-catching cylindrical art museum was designed in the early 1940s by Frank Lloyd Wright (1867-1959, a mighty good innings) who sadly died before its completion. Lloyd Wright designed over a thousand structures in his lifetime and was known for his original and innovative creations, although the first time his name was implanted in my callow brainbox was from the iconic *Bridge Over Troubled Water* album, featuring our old follicly-challenged friends Simon and Garfunkel. The song was called *So Long Frank Lloyd Wright*. I have to say, I never knew whether they were saying goodbye to the bloke or telling us that he was exceedingly tall.

The exterior of the Guggenheim comes as quite a surprise, sitting, as it does, amongst a sea of lofty, oblong and characterless apartment blocks. The building puts me in mind of one of those splendid, but slightly ridiculous, tiered hats worn on Ladies Day at Ascot. The inside is a stark white space-age version of a multi-storey NCP car park without the level floors in between. The unique gallery is on a ramp that rises up from the ground in a continuous spiral along the outer walls of the building, finishing just below the ceiling skylight. As mentioned, there are no horizontal platforms, as such, so it is impossible to say, accurately, how many floors there are due to it being an uninterrupted rising corridor, but, if you forced me to guess, it would be about five floors high.

The museum was currently housing an exhibition of paintings and sculptures by the influential futuristic artist Umberto Boccioni. Born in Italy in 1882, this gifted man was instrumental, through his work, in presenting and popularising the aesthetic quality of the revolutionary futurism movement. In 1916, after a relatively short career, Umberto was drafted into the Italian Army.

Shortly afterwards, he suffered a tragic accident during a cavalry exercise when he was trampled by his own horse and died from his injuries. He was thirty-three years old. I find it somewhat ironic that, as one of the chief standard bearers of futurism, he was cruelly robbed at such a tender age of his very own future, and, more to the point, what a dreadful waste of an extraordinary talent.

I am not a lover of this particular art movement (give me a wishy-washy watercolour every day) but some of this man's paintings blew me away with their depth of colour, hidden meaning and complexity that he managed to incorporate into his work. Unlike Picasso's not dissimilar style, for instance, there was a softness in Boccioni's paintings which sat comfortably with my more conventional artistic leanings.

With another iconic New York venue ticked off my list, the rest of my day was spent counting the hours to when Deb would return from Toronto later that evening. For some inexplicable reason, I had an uncomfortable feeling in my stomach throughout the afternoon that I couldn't explain.

At five p.m., the phone in my apartment rang. I surprised myself by the speed at which I leapt across the room to pick up the receiver.

'Chris? It's Amy.' My heart missed a few beats. Why is Amy calling me? Why is a panicky sounding Amy calling me?

'Amy? What's wrong?'

'I don't know where Deb is. I'm really worried; she just disappeared. I'm calling from the plane and we will be taking off soon and she's not on it,' she said, sounding breathless.

'What do you mean, she just disappeared?' My imagination went into overtime. Had she collapsed? Had she been attacked – kidnapped? My heart was now racing around my ribs.

'Shall I get off the plane, Chris? What should I do?' Amy asked.

'If she's not on the plane with you, yes, I want you to get off and find out where she is, but, first of all, tell me what happened.'

'We joined adjacent lines to go through passport control but my line was moving a bit faster and I got through before Deb. So, I waited for her on the other side but when she hadn't appeared for over five minutes I thought we must have missed each other and that Deb had already boarded the plane,' she said, now close to tears.

Worryingly, Amy had no logical explanation as to the disappearance of my wife. The situation was bizarre in the extreme. I can't begin to tell you how concerned and helpless

I felt at that moment. I put my practical head on. 'Right, I'll try to get her on her mobile. I'll ring you back,' I told her.

Confused, I waited as her phone rang and rang. Just as I expected it to go to voicemail, a frightened voice answered. 'Chris. I've been detained in an interrogation room by customs officials.'

Before I had a chance to reply to the short, hurried message the phone went dead. I tried to ring her back but it went immediately to voicemail.

I then phoned Amy and informed her of the situation. She had already got off the plane and promised me she would wait until my wife reappeared. This gave me a small amount of comfort but I was still worried as to why she had fallen foul of airport security. The thought that made me go cold was that perhaps someone had smuggled some drugs into Deb's hand luggage?

I sat with my mobile clasped tightly in my hand. I stood. I sat again. I then found myself pacing up and down the wooden floor of the apartment, my head spinning with negative thoughts. I plonked myself down again looking at everything in the room and taking in nothing. An agonising half hour crawled by. Silence.

Then the phone rang. I wiped the perspiration from the earpiece and pushed the green icon. 'Chris, I'm OK. I'm with Amy now. There's another plane in fifteen minutes. We've managed to get on that,' she said.

'What happened?'

'It was all to do with my Canadian passport again. I'll fill you in on everything when I get back.'

When Deb arrived back at the apartment at eight thirty p.m., she looked wrung out and totally bemused by her experience. I sat her down and, as the English do in times of distress, made a cup of tea.

'So, come on. What happened?' I asked, bursting to know the details.

Curled up on the sofa and with cup in hand, she began. 'When I handed over my Canadian passport to the female customs officer she asked me, for some unknown reason, how long had I lived in Canada. I told her I didn't live in Canada but was born there and moved to England as a baby.

'Then she said, "What are you doing entering the USA from Canada, then?" I explained I'd been working in the States and had come to Canada on an overnight business trip and was returning to New York to continue my work. Her tone now started to get really hostile. "Where is your proof that you have been working in New York? I need to see a letter of permission," she demanded in front of everyone. It was so embarrassing.'

I had been listening to all this with an increasingly slack jaw. 'Letter of permission?'

'Chris, it gets worse. I went on to explain that I worked for a company in London who has a New York office and that I was here for ninety days to train some US staff. Apparently, this was the worst thing I could have said.

'"Who told you you could work in the USA for ninety days?" she fired at me. By now I was getting really scared and confused by this bully. She was being really horrible. I told her I thought that was the maximum I was allowed to work here. Whoops! Wrong again. As soon as the words left my mouth I was whisked away, like some illegal immigrant or bogus asylum seeker, by this huge, hard-nosed customs officer where he and another female officer grilled me for over an hour. They were really aggressive.'

I sat dumbfounded by this tale of heavy-handedness. 'They didn't hurt you, did they?' I asked.

'No, not really. I was grabbed by the arm and marched off to a building behind passport control and kept locked-up in a small one tiny-windowed room.'

I could only imagine how threatened and afraid she must have felt whilst, most likely, half a dozen enemies of the State were waltzing freely through their misguided hands and into their country.

After realising that they had not, indeed, caught Osama Bin Laden disguised as a well-dressed business woman with an impeccable English accent, they released, with no hint of enthusiasm, my poor quivering wife as though they were doing her a favour.

'I thought we were allies, not enemies, of the United States,' Deb added, climbing wearily to her feet. 'Maybe if I wasn't wearing that false beard and moustache...?'

A harrowing day, stuffed full of jangly nerves and uncertainty was part-placated by some fine wine, hamburger and chips and some serious cuddling. I decided, as we surrendered to a well-earned slumber, that I was getting too old for this crisis lark.

~~

I had decided a few days ago, whilst discovering the small village on Upper East Side, to take Deb there at the weekend and that's where we found ourselves. It was a pretty cool area with some unusual stores. One such shop contained intriguing looking furniture and carefully placed items that would not have been out of place in an eighteenth century coaching inn.

This area was one of the most affluent neighbourhoods in New York City and was once known, fittingly, as the Silk Stocking District. Most members of New York's upper-class families have had residences on the East Upper Side, including the Roosevelts, the Kennedys, the Rockefellas, the Carnegies and the Vanderbilts, amongst the many.

A few streets further up and overlooking the East River was Carl Schurz Park, which housed the Archibald Gracie Mansion – the official residence of the Mayor of the City of New York. Gracie was a Scottish born shipping magnate who in 1799 had a two-storey Colonial style wooden mansion erected as his country residence. Distinguished guests included American President John Quincy Adams and Louis Phillippe, the future King of France.

As a small matter of interest Archibald's great grandson, Archie the fourth, military officer and writer, was one of the lucky few, unlike Astor, who survived the sinking of the Titanic in 1912. I bet *he* wasn't travelling in Steerage! Whilst we're on the subject, here's a rather surprising fact in progressive, modern thinking America. It was a strict rule, and still is, as far as I know, that only visiting public officials and the Mayor's family are allowed to reside with the Mayor at Gracie Mansion.

As a result Mayor Giuliani (1994-2001), one of the most respected of the city's mayors, was not allowed to have his partner live with him in the mansion as they were not married and it would have violated using a taxpayer-funded home for a private citizen. So, poor old Rudy was, I guess, forced to meet his girlfriend in dark alleys and deserted parks whenever the desire arose for a swift, surreptitious coupling. But I'm sure he must have slipped her in through the back entrance (for want of a better phrase) on the occasional cloud-covered night when no-one was looking.

~~

We had a curry last night and it tasted delicious. The trouble is, they always do because all the strong heady spices used can often mask any possible ingredients that may be, how can I say this, not up to scratch. I visited the toilet five times before I dared to leave the apartment with Deb. Feeling a bit more settled and a good deal lighter we headed for the East River again to breathe in some much needed air in an open space that I hoped would clear my senses from last night's mixture of Guinness and chicken dhansak.

We found a seat next to the *dog pound*, a wire-fenced enclosure on the bank of the river, where owners can visit and let their hounds run themselves silly without straying out into the road or plunging into the passing torrent. We were the only people present and there was only one dog. The cute little thing was sitting in the corner of the pound wearing a rather forlorn look on its face. Strangely, the animal was without any sign of an owner. It had, seemingly, taken itself for a walk, entered through the open gate of the concrete playground for dogs and was waiting for a few mates to turn up. Well, that's what it looked like.

As I started toward the small furry beast, thinking it may be lost, injured or abandoned, an old lady arrived with a slightly larger dog. Unleashed, it raced towards me with a disconcerting look of hunger on its face. Just when I was convinced that I was to be his lunch, fortunately it swerved past me in a cloud of dust and skidded to a halt next to the little four-legged sweetie in the corner. Without so much as a by-your-leave or a *do you mind looking the other way, please* it launched itself onto its back and proceeded to copulate furiously with the timorous animal. Thankful that one of my limbs had not disappeared down the throat of this beast, I left them to it and approached the old lady.

'Do you know whose dog that is?' I asked politely, as I pointed to the ball of fluff that was now being rogered with alarming vigour against the wire netting by her lust-crazed hound.

'No, but it's here every Sunday morning. I call her Daisy and Vernon loves to play with her,' she replied, innocently. *You don't say*, I thought, as Vernon, who now had an evil grin all over his slavering chops, was *playing* the living daylights out of poor Daisy. But then I thought, hang on. If Daisy turns up at the same time every Sunday morning, she must realise she is going to get a good seeing-to from Vern the manic canine Casanova. So my feelings of sympathy turned to those of admiration. Good luck to little, lonely Daisy and good luck to the old lady who obviously relishes the sight of her boy getting stuck into the local talent every week.

During this episode of doggy dogging my wife's demeanour had gone from startled to amused and through to giggling. She now wore a playful countenance. 'Don't even think about it,' I said, still feeling weak from the morning's shenanigans.

I don't know, the things you see when you're out minding your own business.

After watching the very public sex show and feeling a little envious of Vernon's staying power, we embarked on an extended riverside walk until my insides started to bubble and gurgle like an old washing machine. I knew immediately that I had to return home. I made it back, just, with sweat running freely from my forehead and by walking with very small steps in the manner of Charlie Chaplin. I made a note, as I dived into the toilet, never again to mix those two ingredients.

Chapter Eleven

During breakfast this morning one half of my lower left molar decided to join eight cornflakes and a dribble of milk that lay at the bottom of my breakfast bowl. It's strange that these things always have a habit of occurring when you are away from home. The last time I lost a tooth was over ten years ago, but I take a three month trip to America...

I rang a recommended dentist at nine a.m., who resided up on 79th between Columbus and Amsterdam (the northern extensions of 9th and 10th Avenue) and, miracle of miracles, got an appointment for eleven thirty, later that morning.

A light dusting of clouds sat high in the sky so I decided to walk, knowing that a good portion of the journey would take me through Central Park. The trip, as anticipated, was a joy. It took me just short of an hour and I discovered many hidden pockets of beauty in the park along the way.

When I arrived, I prepared myself to fill out reams of forms, as I did at the doctor's surgery. I wasn't disappointed. Soon after the mind-numbing exercise was completed, I was promptly sat down and made comfortable, if one can ever be comfortable in a dentist's chair, by a pretty Spanish lady in a spotless white uniform. I guessed she was from Spain by her name tag on her lapel that read Conchita Pasquales and from the few clipped words she spoke when ushering me to the chair.

I leant back against the headrest and began to tell her my predicament until I realised, by virtue of her impassive reaction to my plight, that she hadn't understood a word of what I had just said. She hadn't even bothered to turn around to face me during the unfortunate tale of my oral malfunction. I began to have serious misgivings in granting gob-foraging rights to someone who had access to vicious weapons such as needles, drills and pliers (do dentists still use pliers?) whilst having no means of communicating with me.

Just as I was thinking perhaps I could last another two months without a full complement of hampsteads, a haughty, middle-aged brute of a woman, it was Shrek with tits, swept into the room. 'Why are you sitting in my chair?' she demanded.

At first I thought I had jumped my turn before it struck me that this fearsome creature hovering over me was the dentist. The prospect of being treated by the Spanish assistant suddenly looked more appealing. I stared up at her enormous face and said nothing.

The female hulk bent forward, looked over her heavy-rimmed glasses deep into my eyes and said, 'What seems to be the problem?'

'It's my leg,' I announced, with a wince. She frowned, not picking up on my attempt at dry humour. I waited... nothing. 'OK! I give in. It's my tooth. So, when I explained that my mouth now contained just thirty-one and a half pearlies and not the full compliment with which I arrived on these shores, she nodded and got down to work. After a few prods from her highly qualified, rubber-coated fingers, injections were administered and I was left for ten minutes to go numb.

When she returned, she asked me if my mouth did, in fact, feel numb. 'Yeshthrrffpp,' came my reply, whilst emitting a considerable amount of drool down my peach towelling bib. After what seemed like hours of high-pitched excavation that felt dangerously close to my brain, I was asked to bite down on a mouthful of goo to shape a replacement. Then, a temporary tooth was wedged and glued in and I was told to return in two weeks, on the 13th, of all dates – not that I'm superstitious – to have my new and shiny molar cap fitted.

The plan, regrettably, was to last only until I arrived home after a long walk in much discomfort from my transitory tooth. A soothing swish of my tongue was all it took for it to pop out of its ill-fitting birth. A quick, terse phone call to the dentist found me repeating the now wearisome trudge back uptown to get it shaved and stuck once more onto a now very sore gum. Having given Shrek a prize-withering look, I set off on my journey home once more.

By the time I arrived, I had been traipsing up and down Manhattan for four hours and I felt, excuse the chosen colour of the language, absolutely fucked. I must have covered close to fifteen miles and for what? To get sore feet, an aching jaw and a pair of paralysed lips that felt like two pork sausages.

Mercifully, by six p.m., my chin no longer felt like a piece of mahogany and my mouth had started to work again. Confidence returned, I shambled on tired limbs to 36th and 5th where I met Deb and Amy in a loud and lively pub called The Ginger Man. The watering-hole was named after the racy novel by J.P. Donleavy which was originally banned in America. Due to shifting moral standards it is now regarded as a masterpiece and modern classic. How times change, eh?

We sat in the rear lounge area on sofas where the girls giggled heartily at my half-day dentathon story and I was just thankful that I could speak again. I proceeded to drink beer at a rate that offered rapid relief from my pain.

~~

At seven thirty a.m., the world outside my window was alive with industry and expectation as the inhabitants of this financial giant emerged from their homes – each one forming the pulsating mosaic that was New York City.

I ventured out to get my daily paper and having looked the correct way onto 2nd Avenue to see that the traffic lights were red, started to cross. As I stepped out onto the road I very nearly got run over by a Hispanic looking fellow riding his bike the wrong way down this one-way thoroughfare. Luckily, I saw him out of the corner of my eye and managed to sway back just in time, but not quick enough to avoid the corner of his elbow giving my unsuspecting nose a passing swipe.

'Oi! You little sod, watch where you're going!' I shouted after him. This was immediately followed by, 'If you haven't noticed, you're going the wrong bloody way!' My protestations were met with a sheepish grin as his diminutive legs, which were a circuitous blur, peddled him towards his destination.

This city, if I've not mentioned it before, is full of Chinese and Puerto Ricans riding bicycles. Mostly, they are delivery men or simply part of the everyday traffic racing around the streets in whichever fashion they choose. These irritating little so-and-so's have absolutely no regard for traffic lights, one-way streets, cars or people, and the concept of putting a bell on a bike doesn't seem to have made it over here yet. The NYPD, who are supposed to be a tough, uncompromising police force, appear, surprisingly, to turn a blind eye to these dangerous flouters of the Highway Code. They obviously have bigger fish to fry – like those vicious bastards who get in the wrong lane at toll booths. * (This will make sense further on in the story).

It has been said by many westerners over the years that Chinese people all look the same. This observation, of course, is a wild exaggeration of the facts and deemed, in these times of political correctness, to be extremely racist. They do, of course, have similar characteristics to each other but then so do a lot of other nations around the world.

But, I have to say, every male Puerto Rican that I have come across in this city looks exactly the same. In fact, I'm beginning to think that maybe there is only one individual from that country over here and he's stalking me. Seriously though, they are all five feet two, olive-skinned, with a broad jaw, straight black hair and possess a wide smile crammed full of big shiny teeth. It's the eyes that worry me, however: they have within them a look of mistrust and insecurity that I guess is a reflection of their tough past and how they are treated over here.

Mind you, it would harm their reputation none if they perhaps paused at a stop sign every so often which would avoid scaring the life out of us pedestrians.

The small island of Puerto Rico came under Spanish rule from the late fifteenth century after Christopher Columbus shimmied onto the shores of the modest but attractive

Caribbean island, threw off his hat, swept back his curly locks and declared in his moment of self-approbation, 'This'll do nicely!' The slavery-imposed reign continued for four hundred years until Spain ceded the archipelago to the United States as a result of its defeat in the Spanish-American War of 1898. It was twenty years later that the islanders were granted US citizenship. Eighty-six years after that, they decided in their droves to roll up in Manhattan and jump on the nearest bike with the sole purpose of being a bleedin' nuisance.

I have to add that they all seem to me to be honest, hard-working members of the community, but if one of them ever felt inclined to rob a bank, he would be almost impossible to catch because all his male countrymen would answer to the description of the perpetrator.

I spent the rest of the day stroking my bruised nose and composing three songs for Ryan and Amy's wedding from all the information I had gleaned separately from each of them and their friends. They have, very bravely, allowed me to write and perform songs with my guitar aimed at taking the mickey out of both of them at their impending wedding reception. I am happy with the way the ditties are progressing. This upcoming performance was much welcomed, giving me an important assignment, a written target, with time constraints.

A good while later, a portion of freshly cooked salmon sat comfortably in my stomach as I lay in bed next to my wife and listened to another day in my American adventure come to a rain-dribbling close.

~~

I stood watching in fascination a fine spray of rain lacquer my apartment windows, forming occasional globules, which eventually gained the necessary bulk to zigzag their way down the glass in an uncertain, stop-start journey to the sill. This liquefied downward-only version of snakes and ladders was hypnotising. Nevertheless, I prayed the clouds responsible would soon run out of water so I could continue my fact-finding mission around the symmetrical streets of Manhattan.

I skulked around the apartment until late morning when I felt as if I would burst with boredom. The miserable weather continued. My mind began to wander. I even wondered what it was like to be Vernon. He lived in a completely different world from me, one where he never had to work for a living, was always loved, fed and watered and, above all else, existed in an accepted environment where he could get his leg over whenever the urge gripped him and with any bit of stuff he took a fancy to. I could never understand the phrase *It's a dog's life*, which was meant to portray one of hardship.

I used the rest of the day to write and practise my songs for tomorrow's performance, but, during the evening, I sensed a butterfly or two sprouting wings in my stomach; I was beginning to have doubts as to whether my Yankee audience would tune in to my English-bred sense of humour. This could be an embarrassing disaster.

~~

Today is the day of the wedding. I spent most of the morning putting the finishing touches to my songs. Then I realised that I needed a music stand. 'Where could I hire one?' I asked myself. The answer, of course, was that I hadn't a clue! Out on the streets I emerged, dipping into hardware stores and record shops but with no luck.

Ah, but then:

'A music stand, buddy?' said the young and surprisingly helpful assistant in the enormous Barnes and Noble bookshop. 'You want 44th and 9th – Luthier Music.'

So I thanked him and departed. I traipsed past Grand Central Station, skipped though Three Times Square, swerved around the busy Port Authority Bus Terminal and arrived in... the land time forgot.

What a strange area 44th and 9th was! To traverse through street after street of cacophonous traffic, filter myself through a scuttling of pedestrians and then turn a corner to find I'm in Tombstone, Arizona was, to say the least, startling. I swear I could hear the distant and haunting toll of a bell as I passed deserted roads and desolate buildings looking for this one shop that would provide my needs. But there it was, at 341 West 44th street, in all its chocolate-brown blind and shop front glory – Luthier Music Corp in big white letters.

I pushed the advert-card-covered door open to the sound of a tinkling bell and ventured in amongst the endless rows of shiny guitars, which hung enticingly from steel hooks on painted walls. After negotiating myself around various sets of pearly-waistcoated drum kits I arrived at a small, untidy desk.

'Hi! I'd like to hire a music stand please?' I asked the pony-tailed assistant.

'No problem, man,' he replied, instantly picking up on my gender. After showing me a small selection of used stands pulled from raggedy boxes I made my choice. That'll be thirty dollars and needs to be back by Monday,' said laidback Larry.

''Scuse me? How much? Thirty bucks for a music stand? I could bring it back tomorrow,' I replied, hopefully. It cut no ice. He went on to tell me that that was the standard charge for equipment hire. 'So, I could have a Fender Stratocaster for the same money then?' I stated, somewhat taken aback.

'Yeh, with a holding deposit, yeh,' he replied matter-of-factly.

'Hang on,' I said, getting my retired money-broking brain into gear, 'what does a new one of these cost?'

'This one? Erm…' He turned slower than is possible without stopping, drifted over to his computer and punched in a few numbers. 'Twenty-three bucks,' he said, with a hint of embarrassment spreading over his unshaven face.

'Ooh! What a dilemma,' I replied. Twenty-three dollars flew out of my pocket before I could say, *do I look stupid* and off I strolled with my own brand new music stand.

Back in the apartment I set up my shiny stand with my typed words and practiced my act for the next three hours until Deb arrived home at five thirty p.m. Shortly after, we caught a cab down town to the Tribeca Rooftop, which was on the corner of Canal Street and Hudson Street. This was, I discovered later, an extremely popular and not inexpensive wedding venue. When we stepped from the lift onto the twelfth floor I could see why.

'Stunning,' was the first word that Deb and I exchanged as we walked across the highly polished cherry-wood dance floor. The room was as big as an Olympic size swimming pool and sat beneath a magnificent sixty-five foot long skylight.

The enormous picture windows on three sides of the room afforded breathtaking views over the Hudson River. Rows of white linen-covered circular tables, seductively lit, were laid with style and attention to detail.

The only thing that I needed to do now was to locate the two mikes and mike stands, one for voice and one for guitar. I was told they would be there for me on arrival. After consulting the manager and MC for the evening I realised that no such stands existed. Oh, shit! My nerves, which were just beginning to behave themselves, were now screaming and running around like five-year-olds in an unsupervised crèche. I had just two hours before I was due to perform. This was not good. I was surrounded by blank and don't blame me looks until the DJ sauntered over and said, 'I hear you need a couple of mikes and stands.'

'Yes,' I said, in desperation, 'and if you can help me I'll have your babies and even pay for their maintenance.' This guy, who I could have kissed if he had been my type and was not wearing a goatee, took the trouble to go all the way back home, collect the said items and return, all within the hour. What a splendid fellow.

When the crowd, which numbered one hundred and forty, were all seated the wedding party, about thirty, who were all corralled together upstairs, were introduced to the rest of us by the DJ. One by one they paraded down the sweeping staircase to a background tape of showtime music in a ridiculously grand manner as if they were the stars of a Broadway show. It took all my self control and, by the look of it, Deb's too, not to burst out laughing at this ridiculously flamboyant parade of aunts, uncles, grandparents and wannabe celebs. Especially, when having descended the stairs, each one performed a brief dance, shimmy or pirouette to the pounding beat and obvious delight of the clapping and whooping American audience.

Deb and I, the only English faces in the crowd, sat astonished as the soccer crowd-like assembly rose to an ear-tingling crescendo when the bride and groom finally made their grand appearance. It was all quite bizarre but, I have to admit, enjoyable in an oh sod it, we may as well join in with all this madness, kind of way. The meal, it had to be said, was delicious and bountiful.

At ten p.m., as the coffees, chocs and liqueurs were being ingested, I started my act. My first song was about Ryan, sung to the tune of Frank Sinatra's *My Way* and went down very well to enthusiastic applause. I then moved on to Amy. This was the first time that I had played to a 'foreign' audience and I was still not sure they would sign in to my brand of mickey-taking humour, but again they clapped and whooped.

I then launched into my final song, one of my own melodies, about the both of them. The content, once again, highlighted their quirks and foibles, gleaned from friends and from themselves on separate occasions. After the first verse, I noticed a few polite smiles on the faces around me and the thought crossed my mind that this intimate ditty might be too near the knuckle.

I needn't have worried. By the second verse, the guest-filled tables were rocking under the weight of very welcome laughter whilst Ryan and Amy, thank goodness, appeared to be bathing happily in their musical dose of adverse publicity. When I finished I received a standing ovation from the entire room and for the rest of the evening I was showered with enough compliments to stuff a pillow. I had done it. My home-bred musical waggery had been accepted by this overseas audience. I was elated.

Interestingly, I was offered work there and then by a few of the guests and told by one high-ranking executive that if I was to stay in New York, I could make a very healthy living performing this kind of act on the corporate circuit. Tempting, I thought, but tonight my act was over; I was now able to relax and make a concerted attempt to catch up with the champagne-soaked smiling faces.

I have to say, it was very brave of Ryan and Amy to allow an alien and virtual stranger to perform such a personal and risky act at what was going to be the most important day of their lives. As I am writing this, ten years later, the thought has just entered my head for the first time – what if it had been a disaster? Me, the wife and the guitar would have been lucky to get out of the place in one piece. And I really like that guitar.

My lasting memory of that night was of Amy's mum looking like she was on the edge of a nervous breakdown for the whole duration of the party. Actually, that's not my lasting memory. The image which will probably never leave me was of her boyfriend, a sixty-five-year-old Vincent Price lookalike, who turned up with his pet poodle in a shopping basket.

~~

Most of the morning was spent on the internet trying to book a four-day break in Boston or Rhode Island, both of which seemed like an interesting getaway location. Every hotel was either full, ridiculously expensive, ugly or all three.

Is it me or does everyone else experience the feeling that their head is about to explode after anything more than an hour of a fruitless search on the World Wide Web. My temples constrict, my back and neck lose all mobility, my backside goes numb and I turn into an impatient imbecile. Screaming helps but tends to scare the neighbours.

After lunch we decided to have a peek inside the Trump Tower (5th Avenue between 56th and 57th). The interior, bathed beneath seductive lighting, was clad in a pink, white-veined marble which, I discovered later, had the swanky name of Breccia Pernice, who I could've sworn played left back for AC Milan. The vast walls were bedecked with brass fittings and huge mirrors. My initial impression was that the whole interior had been sprayed with gold – but it was more over-the-top ostentatious than oh-so-cool opulence.

Donald, he of the comb-over, is the son of Fred (1905-1999), a wealthy New York City real-estate developer, and Mary MacLeod, who hailed from the Isle of Lewis off the west coast of Scotland. He was given control of his father's company in 1971 and is now estimated to be worth from anything up to seven billion dollars. The actual figure seems to be the subject of constant speculation.

He has, more than once and to my surprise, shown an interest in being a candidate for the Presidency of the United States. If this ever came to fruition the ongoing discussions over the true amount of his fortune would soon cease as all Presidential candidates are required to disclose their personal finances. Whatever onward path he chooses to take, it is safe to say that Fred's little offspring has been pretty successful and

168

won't be queuing up for social welfare benefits in the near future.

*Since writing this book Mr D Trump has become President of the United States of America. Wow!

Its next-door neighbour and dwarfed by Mr Trump's Tower was the flagship store of the luxury jeweller's Tiffany and Co. Tiffany's was more US Government building than jewellers but still powerfully impressive. As much as I tried to keep my wife away from the lavish display of gorgeous gems and treasured trinkets she managed to persuade me to wander in and roam amongst most things that glittered *and* were gold but, sadly, proved far too stretchy for my diminutive pocket.

Later that afternoon I was on the cusp of throwing my laptop out of the window when, zip-a-dee-doo-dah, I finally secured a sea-front boutique hotel in a one-horse town called Orleans which was on the elbow of Cape Cod. It took another two hours to book a hire car for the journey. All done and dusted by five p.m. – piece of cake!

When I rang Deb to give her the news, she was ecstatic. She had been under sustained pressure in the office recently and it was just what she needed. At least my arduous efforts were worth it.

~~

Today I was going to traverse across sixty-five streets in an uptown direction to the Marcus Garvey Memorial Park. This was not, particularly, to see the park but to look around the area of Harlem. Before I came to New York I had read about or been told two things concerning the district. The Harlem

Globetrotters, famous and multi-talented basketball team, was the first, whom I had seen perform on my television many years before. The second was the popular advice that I received on my first visit here in 1980: *Don't go there, buddy. It is an African American ghetto and it is dangerous.* The general consensus being that, if you were white-skinned, it was a no-go area. Though, as with any reputation, I had a sneaking suspicion that these rumours were subject to exaggeration and political bias.

But from the 1960s to the early '90s, a good deal of that bad publicity was warranted. That was until Mayor Giuliani initiated a campaign to clean up the area. The mayor's introduction of a greater police presence and a zero-tolerance policy proved to be a great success. In the mid-sixties the drug addiction rate in Harlem was ten times that of the New York City average and half the children in the area grew up with one parent (mostly the mother) or none at all. The crime rate was reported as being fifty per cent higher than that of the entire NYC area.

From 1990-2008, crime in Harlem, due to Giuliani's aggressive policing, dropped like a stone – murder fell by eighty percent, robbery seventy-three percent, burglary eighty-six percent and rape fifty-eight percent. Although the district had undergone a significant improvement, unemployment was still a major problem and today crime still remains higher than the rest of New York City.

With a measure of lukewarm disquiet settling in my stomach, I set off on my four mile journey uptown to Harlem. My route took me along Lexington Avenue, which runs parallel to the East Side of Central Park. When I reached 110th

Street, the park ceased to be and I found myself in the area known as Spanish Harlem, which, despite its name, is not considered to be part of Harlem at all.

Similarly, however, this working class location had a disturbing history of high unemployment, teenage pregnancy, AIDS and drug abuse. Two thirds of the adults in this location were reported as overweight or obese and the area had the highest violent crime rate in Manhattan. The asthma figures here, amongst both children and adults, was reported to be five times the national average. This was blamed on rodent and roach infestation, smoke, dust and mould-covered damp walls due to poor living conditions, which in twenty-first century New York is a scandal.

The neighbourhood is predominantly Puerto Rican and Latin American, with a growing element of Asian inhabitants, but, in the 1870s, the area was known as Italian Harlem when a large number of Southern Italian and Sicilian immigrants moved in, soon to be dominated by organised crime syndicates. I can't deny that the knowledge I had of this quarter's colourful history did put my senses on high alert as I passed through the district. As it was, the locals ignored my presence whilst the shops and general ambience, from what I could see, were not much different from most other regions I had visited on this trip.

The buildings here were as attractive as any I had witnessed in Manhattan, the streets were clean and the people seemed amiable enough. My journey took me past famous haunts, such as the Art Deco style Lenox Lounge on Lenox Avenue, the continuation of 6th Avenue between 124th and 125th. The bar was founded in 1939 and presented many great jazz artists such as Billie Holiday and Miles Davis. The area, as far as restaurants were concerned, was going through somewhat of a renaissance. More varied and upmarket eateries were opening, bringing in financial investment and much needed employment to the area.

125th Street bears the title of Martin Luther King Boulevard, which is a good deal wider than most of the streets in downtown Manhattan and regarded as the Main Street of Harlem. Along this thoroughfare stand such noted buildings as the Hotel Theresa, the Studio Museum of Harlem and the Apollo Theatre.

The Hotel Theresa was built in 1912 by German stockbroker Gustavus Sidenberg and he named it after his wife, Ethel. Just joking. Sandwiched between lowly red-brick and brownstone structures its white terracotta facade struck a dramatic spectacle. In 1960, it housed the straggly-bearded face of the Cuban Prime Minister, Fidel Castro, when he came to the opening session of the United Nations and, in October of that year, John F Kennedy used the hotel in his campaign for the Presidency.

Many such dignitaries, too numerous and frankly too boring to mention, have passed through the doors of the stately hotel. After such an impressive past history it has now, sadly, lost its pomp. It's presently used as an office building and has been renamed Theresa Towers, which sounds to me like a hairy-armed Spanish shot-putter.

The Studio Museum in Harlem, a contemporary art museum devoted to the work of African American artists, was founded in 1968 and moved to its present location in 1977. Its design has all the hallmarks of that era; square, flat-faced and uninspiring. The exhibits inside, I've been told, are the antithesis of this. Curiously, this is often the case. Many modern art venues, I have found, filled with displays of thought-provoking and innovative work tend to have the most unimaginative and dull exteriors – the Hyde Park Art Centre in Chicago being the perfect example.

The Apollo Theatre was built in 1914 as Hurtig and Seamon's New Burlesque Theatre. It became the Apollo in 1934, when it first opened to black patrons. In 1983 both the interior and exterior of the building was added to the National Register of Historic Places. This piece of knowledge came as somewhat of a surprise as I stood across the road eyeing the exterior. The extended, square advertising plinth that hovered over the entrance gave it the look of many a bog-standard cinema you would find shoe-horned between a row of high street shops in any English town. The crimson-seated interior, though, was a delight. The architecture of the three-tiered auditorium was as captivating as any of London's West End theatres.

From 1987 to 2008 Showtime at the Apollo, a popular television variety show presenting new talent, was broadcast from the venue. Stars of film and TV Bill Cosby and Richard Prior are reported to have cut their comedic teeth on Apollo's stage, which also launched the career of a seventeen-year-old called Ella Fitzgerald. It is estimated that some 1.3 million people visit the Apollo each year. And in 2004 I was one of 'em.

A few short pavements away sat the twenty acres of Marcus Garvey Park, which acts as a massive square roundabout plonked smack in the middle of 5th Avenue and bordered by 120th and 124th Street. It was named after the Jamaican born publisher and crusader for Black Nationalism. Like most other parks in this city it provided an immediate open and green escape from its highly populated, urban environment.

On my visit it was full of picnickers, dog walkers and joggers. There were two playgrounds, an amphitheatre and a swimming pool on the ground floor level but the elevated section (a bit of a no-go area) is, apparently, a haunt for prostitutes and drug dealers, which is a great shame as it is full of nooks and crannies on winding, varied levels that would be every child's idea of heaven.

This was where my excursion into Harlem ended. The late afternoon light was beginning to fade and I had a long walk home.

Deb, similar to myself, was aware of the reputed dangers lurking in this infamous district and had been worried about my safety all day, bless her. That was until I met her after work, unmolested and in a fettle that was as fine as she could have wished for. I was thrilled to reveal to her that my Harlem experience was one of relaxed enjoyment.

On the way home we decided to have a quiet plate of pasta in a bog-standard, boring looking diner just a two-minute walk from our apartment. The place was called Mimi's and was similar to a thousand other eateries with large square windows and cheap seafront cafe tables and chairs within. But here's where I say that you shouldn't judge a book by its cover.

The middle-aged waitress was a real live-wire – big girl with a personality to match. Then there was Hunter Blue. He was the pianist, positioned just inside the front entrance. My first impression was that he made Liberace look like an old stick-in-the-mud. He was stark raving mad. He had a collection of hooters, horns and whistles and donned an assortment of flashing headgear whenever he felt the urge to entertain the customers. This was carried out with a constant deadpan, bored-to death expression and brilliant piano playing skills that covered a ridiculously wide range of musical categories. When he sang, which was only on rare occasions, he bore a remarkable resemblance to an effeminate Mae West.

He was, of course, very gay with an over-the-top deep South American accent. His head, totally devoid of hair, was covered from time to time with one of his hilarious wigs. We sat alongside his piano after our meal and I introduced Deb and myself. He then made a big show of announcing to the rest of the patrons that he had two people from England roosting on his stools. He stood, saluted and proceeded to play the British national anthem to the amusement of all, but the highlight of the evening was to come.

There were three people dining on the table next to the piano, to whom Hunter Blue had nodded on their arrival. It turned out that one of them was an American/Italian male opera singer who, we discovered later, had just finished a performance that night at New York City's Metropolitan Opera House. He was accompanied by his wife and his manager. On finishing his meal he was asked if he would like to sing for us by our waggish pianist. We couldn't believe our luck when he said yes.

He proceeded to treat us to various operatic classics with a few contemporary numbers thrown in. His voice was as pure as any I have heard. Maybe if he was on stage with such greats as the 'three tenors' he may have not stood up to comparison but in the confines of a small, faceless food joint it was pure magic. I can't begin to tell you the thrill of witnessing a professional, no further than three feet away, exhibit the control and clarity of voice that his particular craft demands. It moved Deb to tears and the hairs on the back of my neck have never been so erect.

It was the best night of our trip by a mile. We were privileged and extremely lucky though to have picked that particular evening.

Manhattan has this infectious energy that is impossible to ignore and without realising it its irresistible force can gobble you up and galvanise you into becoming a permanent party animal before you can say *fancy an early night and a nice cup of Horlicks*. I guess if we lived here permanently we would pace ourselves and find a routine that was kinder to our vital organs. But with the knowledge lurking in the back of my brain that we were only here on a quarter-year jaunt it seemed a terrible waste to sit in our lovely but bijou apartment every night, TV console in hand, searching for something more educational to watch than ten-year-old episodes of Ground Force.

Now we had something else to look forward to: Boston, Massachusetts.

Chapter Twelve

Our bags were packed. We were ready to go. Standing here outside the door, we were off on our mini Easter holiday and to check out Boston. At seven fifteen a.m., we climbed into a taxi that took us up to 84th between 3rd and Lex – the car hire depot. I signed my name a thousand times on reams of paper with writing too small to read and departed in our economy four-door Ford Astra automatic. I had downloaded directions from MapQuest and now dumped them in my wife's uncertain hands. Cape Cod here we come.

After five minutes of driving a left hand drive car on the 'wrong' side of the road, in a confusing city, surrounded by hurried and discourteous drivers, we arrived at the Triborough Bridge toll booths. The construction of this complex of three separate bridges commenced in 1929, at the onset of the Wall Street Crash. Despite obvious funding problems at such a time of financial uncertainty, it opened to traffic on 11th July 1936.

As I drove slowly towards the booths we were unsure at which short queue of waiting cars we should head for. Some were marked "Cash" and others had wording with which we were not familiar. We assumed the cash would be where you threw a bunch of coins into a bucket, like they do in England. As we had no coins we joined another queue expecting to pay with a note or a credit card. As the car in front produced some sort of pass we realised that we were at the wrong booth. But there was one car behind me so I couldn't reverse back to join the correct one.

As I lowered my window to explain our mistake to the vastly overweight, fast approaching African American traffic policeman he bent forward and launched into a terrifying tirade released from a foot in front of my astonished face.

'Can you read?' he shouted. I opened my mouth to reply. He repeated, even louder, 'Can you read?'

I tried to explain. 'Excuse me. I am English and in England cash means coins. The system is...'

'Can you read? Are you stupid?' he re-spat at me, totally ignoring my attempt at a polite explanation, as he continued his rant.

'It was a simple mistake. What do you want me to do?' I offered. But he was oblivious to anything I said and continued to humiliate me by bellowing a string of insults through the open car window. It was completely out of context with the circumstances.

What was wrong with this imbecile? The temptation to get out of my car and beat him around the head with my rolled up map of America was overwhelming.

Then, to my utter amazement he said he was going to fine me eighty-five dollars for some kind of road violation and demanded my driving licence and car details. He pointed to a small office. 'Pull over there,' he instructed. He disappeared inside with my particulars.

'He can't treat you like this. It's ridiculous,' said Deb, who by this time was crying. Seeing her so upset only doubled my feeling of anger. I could feel myself about to do something stupid that I knew I'd regret, such was this unjust state of affairs we found ourselves in.

The thing is, we have had a long history of friendship with the USA; fought together in wars, never drained their economy as illegal immigrants and have no wish to fly planes into their cities' tall buildings. Yet here I was, being treated like a common criminal! For what? Driving dangerously? Driving drunk? Breaking any laws? No. For joining the wrong fucking queue.

Five minutes later, with steam now pouring out of my little car's windows, he emerged and handed me back my documents and a summons that had to be settled within thirty days. How I held my temper in check, I will never know, but, as I started the car to drive away I couldn't resist an affectionate, 'I am English and proud of it, and I think you'll find that my literacy skills are far in excess of yours... you ignorant fat wanker.' The last bit added in order to bring my insult down to a level that I thought he might understand. I left him mouth agape as we sped off into the rising sun.

By the way, I would like you all to know that I never paid the fine and the summons went straight over the meshed fence of the Triborough Bridge and was last seen floating down the Harlem River.

Such was the tension and pent-up anger in the car it was a good many miles down the road before either one of us spoke. It was Deb. 'Chris, if you hold that steering wheel any tighter you'll break it.' I glanced down at ten white knuckles and for a second I imagined them wrapped around the policeman's throat. 'We're off on holiday and we're not going to let that idiot ruin it, are we?' she added.

I made an effort to loosen my strangle-hold on the wheel. 'You are right, of course... which makes a welcome change!' I replied. We looked at each other, there was a pause, then we both roared with laughter. It was the release we needed. But, in truth and don't tell the missus, it took me hours to calm down completely and as a start to a relaxing holiday, arranged mainly to give Deb a few days relaxation, it sucked. What was all that about?

It took five hours to reach the very striking Sagamore Bridge which ferried us over the Cape Cod Canal that connects Cape Cod to the mainland of Massachusetts. Despite the four-lane roadway over the bridge being rather narrow the design had a striking rainbow-like steel fretwork frame. This appeared, on first impression, to rise up out of the waters of the canal forming a graceful arch across the expanse of liquid before disappearing back into the flow.

The towns we drove through were no less impressive. Such wonderful names as Hyannis, Dennis, Brewster and Chatham slipped comfortably past our car windows with not one high-rise building or gigantic shopping mall to be seen. The houses were mainly two-storey timber built cottages all painted in pastel shades of cream, primrose and eggshell blue and all had lovingly-kept gardens.

Gardens, as if you didn't know, are called *yards* in this part of the world. Hardly the most aesthetically pleasing word to describe the beautiful and brain-healing appendages that Mother Nature provides to soften our dissonant living quarters.

How different would our history be if the Americans had preceded the rest of us featherless bipeds onto this planet? Adam and Eve banished from the Yard of Eden – doesn't quite conjure up any great loss, does it? How long would the queues be to see the beautiful flowers at England's Kew Yards? Pretty short, I'd say. Would the Beatles have been arsed to visit an Octopus's Yard in the shade, whether it was under or above the bloody sea? No, they wouldn't.

The road to our hotel in Orleans threaded us through a constant maze of inlets from the ocean, forming vast mirrored lakes that snaked and dissolved through acres of tall pine trees and lush forest. It truly was a journey to make the soul sing. Our modest hotel was on the shore of one of these inlets and our room's two large picture windows looked out over an enormous sun-streaked lagoon. As I stood, soothed by this unexpected delight, the fetid memory of my encounter with the abusive cop dissolved in an instant. We went to bed bellies full of fried chicken, heads full of expectation and with the lasting vision of the floaty view from our hotel windows.

This morning our shimmering bay was even more beautiful. A soft breeze had encouraged our lake to form gentle ripples across its surface, which acted as an undulating platform for a million sparkling, platinum sprites that danced and skipped across the water like gambolling lambs. After six weeks entombed in New York City, this simple joy was a sight to which words could not do justice.

Showered and reclothed we made our way down the wood-slatted stairs to the dining room with much enthusiasm. This low-ceilinged room was decorated with a daubed-on tobacco-stain-brown emulsion, decked with dark brown tables and chairs and was devoid of even a hint of character. In fact, the only thing present of interest and that didn't come in any shade of brown was me and the wife.

There was no hand-wringing employee to welcome us so we helped ourselves to a buffet breakfast and were in the car by nine thirty a.m. Route 6 took us back to Sagamore Bridge where we hopped onto Route 3 to Boston. We arrived at eleven fifteen a.m., drove over the flyover and... were confronted with New York's sister. Concrete was spread in lavish portions wherever we gawped. By the time we had reached the centre of the city, having been stuck in traffic for fifteen minutes on a dark and depressing underpass all we wanted to do was drive back out again – which is exactly what we did.

We got as far as Quincy, which I'm sure I had as a kid before they ripped out my tonsils, and every instinct in me was urging my foot to stay on the accelerator pedal and hightail it back to our exclusively brown hotel. However, that would have been a touch defeatist and I owed it to Deborah to give it another bash.

So, we parked up in a Thai restaurant car park, had a quick wee in the Dunkin' Donut store next door and asked the manager if there was a better way back into Boston. Whether the Donut manager was deaf, pissed off that we had used his conveniences and weren't going to spend any money in his cheap restaurant I don't know, because my question was met with steely little eyes and a deafening silence.

I turned to look at Deb who looked at me before we returned our gaze to the manager. Still nothing. This situation was surreal. Do I stand there until he tells us to fuck off? Should I buy a donut and try asking again or do I tell him what an ignorant knob he is, swan out and take my question elsewhere? Time stood still and I began to detect the howling of a distant wind as tumbleweed rolled past the window. Then, suddenly, two lovely old ladies who were sitting nearby piped up, 'Take the T (subway train) to Park Station, dear. It's the best way.'

I thanked the ladies and shook a sad head at the manager as we took our leave. On the way to the station I thought, why would anyone make a special effort to be such an objectionable old bugger? Life's too short, surely.

The brief train journey brought us up smack in the middle of Boston Common, which, basically, in UK terms was a public park. Ah! This was better and more of what I expected. We took a walk through the park and up to Beacon Hill named, apparently, due to it being the highest point in central Boston on which there once stood a beacon to warn its people of any approaching invasion.

This area was one of obvious wealth. Row upon row of impressively grand townhouses and fashionable shops lined the streets. These were decked with Victorian type gas lamps, adding to the quaint mood of the well-groomed neighbourhood. I detected a strong English and French influence in the architecture and of the general ambience. Having been surrounded by mostly twentieth century New York for nigh on two months it was a pleasure to be dragged back a few hundred years to where the buildings sat more comfortably on the eye.

Why is that I wonder? Why do old cars, artefacts and ancient structures fill the heart with a frisson of envy, an assured comfortable cosiness that modernity can never match? Beats me! I am aware, as human beings, we are always searching for progress, which is why we ventured from our caves and filled the world with round wheels, electricity and

McDonalds. I just wish our eager architects and town planners could temper the desire to forever clamour for change simply for the sake of change. If something works and looks beautiful, leave it alone.

The highlight of our trip, I'm not ashamed to admit, was having a pint of Boston Ale and a spot of lunch in Cheers, but it was nothing like the bar in the TV programme. We then took ourselves down to Quincy market that did have a replica of sorts of the Cheers bar. The market building was constructed around 1824 and named in honour of the mayor of Boston, Josiah Quincy, previously a member of the US House of Representatives. He organised the construction of the market without incurring any debt or taxes; an achievement, I noted at the time, not to be sniffed at.

The choice of food on display throughout the immaculately kept indoor parade was mind-boggling in the extreme. The cuisine of a host of different countries was displayed with great care and attention on spotless shelves and trays, presented by smiley faces with hopeful pockets.

The market was situated near to the Quayside. At the water's edge we stood peering out onto a twinkling viridian sea as a procession of aeroplanes skimmed over our heads and skidded to a brake-singeing stop at Boston's Logan International Airport. Passengers from Canada, Europe, Asia, Mexico and various uncharted outposts can all fly to Logan direct and, by the look of it, they'd all decided to turn up today.

When I first suggested a trip to Boston to my wife, the nostalgic side of me expected there to be a preserved olde worlde waterfront quarter of this city that paid homage to the Boston Tea Party. You know – a magnificent fully rigged ship tied to a creaky old wooden jetty and a tour-guide kitted out in the dress of the late eighteenth century era. Then, for a fistful of dollars, you would be allowed to clamber around the ship, with the guide filling you in on all the historical sexy bits. However, unless I missed it, no such delights existed in 2004.

The dress of the late eighteenth century? When I wrote that line, it got me thinking. I began to research the popular garb of that period and got some surprises. The men's outfit consisted mainly of shirt, waistcoat, knee breeches and long jacket. Underdrawers were occasionally worn beneath the rough wool or leather breeches but quite often nothing at all, so chafing around the old crown jewels must have been a constant and unwelcome problem.

To be regarded as properly dressed, a silk, linen or cotton neckerchief was fastened over the shirt collar by a buckle. The shirt in those days was considered as an item of underwear and a man was rarely seen without the covering of a waistcoat or jacket. God knows how they managed to breathe and work on hot summer days, especially when regular personal bathing was regarded as popular then as foreign call-centres are today.

Stockings of various materials covered the lower leg and both shoes were *straight lasted* meaning there was no shaping of a left or right shoe – not wonderfully comfortable, I wouldn't have thought. At least you were never going to put them on the wrong feet. Three-cornered and round hats were the norm.

Women's attire started with a linen or cotton shift, which acted as both slip and nightgown. This was worn night and day, often for weeks on end, without laundering the garment. Underpants or knickers did not exist so nothing was worn

185

beneath the shift. Wool or linen stockings came to just above the knee and secured with cloth ties. Up to four petticoats around the waist were added, depending on the weather, and a tight fitting waistcoat on the top with ankle length gowns or skirts to finish.

Similar to the men, personal hygiene was not high on the list of priorities to these working women. Hair was often left unwashed throughout winter before the phial of Head and Shoulders made an appearance. This meant that the nit-infested hair was usually tied back and kept beneath a hat or bonnet.

I don't know about you but the idea of snuggling up close to your loved one in those over-dressed, soap-free times, let alone indulging in a game of hide the sausage, wouldn't really make me rush home after work in a lustful state. But then I guess if personal service history was pretty much similar to all throughout your village – meaning that everyone smelled the same – then game on!

In case you are not particularly au fait with the story of the Tea Party allow me to provide a brief synopsis. Basically, a group of Massachusetts Patriots, called The Sons of Liberty, were not happy about the monopoly on American tea importation granted by the sitting parliament to the East India Company. This was an English owned concern that traded in, amongst others, cotton, salt, tea and opium. The patriots were unhappy at paying a tax on tea that the Americans had not authorised. They wanted to be taxed by their own elected representatives and not by the British Government.

On 16th December 1773, the demonstrators, disguised as Indians, which strikes me as a rather odd thing to do, destroyed the entire supply of tea (three hundred and forty odd chests), sent by the East India Company, by tossing the cargo straight into the sea. The British Government responded aggressively, as you would expect, and the episode escalated into the American Revolution, where thirteen colonies in North America joined forces to break away from the British Empire, combining to become the United States of America. The dumping of the forty-five tons of tea, estimated to be a million dollars worth in today's market, was a brave and seminal moment in America's history.

Back in Orleans we dined at a restaurant bar called The Binnacle. I knew the name had some sort of nautical connection but I had to look it up on my laptop dictionary. For those of you bereft of sea-going legs, a binnacle is a non-magnetic stand for a ship's compass. The décor, not surprisingly, was dripping with fishing nets, anchors, ship's wheels, sextants, telescopes and a dose of scurvy for those who wanted a few weeks off work. Then it was back to our hotel to rest our heads and dream of what delights old Cape Cod would deliver us on the morrow.

~~

At breakfast, we found a table in our snuff-coloured dining room tucked around a hidden corner, next to a window that had much the same view as our hotel room. There we had another buffet-type meal accompanied by the sight of the tranquil, bespangled lagoon. It made the muesli more harmonious, it caused the fresh orange juice to sing but, sadly, failed to improve the insipid sausages that were a mixture of lumps of fat and compressed cardboard wrapped in a condom.

Why, I ask, is nearly every sausage in the civilised world stuffed with such insalubrious shit? If someone fell upon the idea of filling these semi-flaccid cylinders only with top quality pork, flavoured with savoury herbs and spices, then charged a raised but appropriate price, I'm convinced they would sell like hot cakes. How excited would we all feel to then realise that they weren't actually cakes at all, but posh, healthy bangers?

Having performed the things you do after a greasy breakfast and before going on a trip out in the car, we escaped once more into the wilds of the Cape. Draped in a cerulean blue sky we propelled ourselves along the snaky ten mile drive to Chatham. If the Cape is viewed as a bent arm then Chatham is on the point of the elbow. The town was not much more than one main high street, possibly a quarter of a mile in length – called, appropriately, Main Street.

It was a glorious day and the predominantly white painted, wood-panelled Colonial style houses set against the clear blue sky were, initially, a joy to witness. It was obvious that the residents here took great care and no little pride in their shiny little village. It was perfect. In truth, it was almost too perfect. It was very white; brilliant white, in fact. The words twee and aseptic hovered in the air above the rows of shiny blue-grey tiled roofs.

If that sounds a bit harsh on the parochial efforts of the Chathamites, then so be it. I'm not convinced that it's healthy or natural for anyone's neighbourhood to be kept so flawless, so utterly immaculate. Pretty and cute and scrubbed is for babies and kittens. As far as I'm concerned character, quirky and a light dusting of rough edges is far more pleasing on the soul and the eye – and that goes for towns, villages and women. I'm surprised there wasn't a sign at the entrance to Chatham stating: *Would all visitors please remove their shoes when entering our village and leave them by this sign, where you can collect them on your exit. Thank you for your visit.*

I wondered if all the dogs and cats were made to wear nappies. Just imagine if you were caught dropping litter in a place like this – you'd never make it out of the place alive.

When my wife stopped to look in a shop window, I whispered, 'Keep moving!'

'Why?' she said, frowning.

'Cos if we don't, we may get spray-painted white.'

It was that type of place.

On first appearance, the street looked to be lined with a row of white, chocolate-box houses, but, as we drew nearer, they turned out to be shops – all with pristine gabled frontages and white picket-fenced lawns that you could eat your dinner off. We took many photos of the buildings and the magnificent wood built churches (painted white, of course). This community did love a church – they seemed to be everywhere. There were three just on Main Street and I'm going to reveal their varied history.

The First Congregational Church was erected, first time around, in 1690. Coincidentally, it was the same year that the first paper money appeared in America, and, would you believe, it appeared from just down the road. The notes were issued by the nearby English chartered Massachusetts Bay Company as promises to pay American troops to fight the

French in Canada. Each piece of paper represented a coin's worth which could be redeemed for "real money" (coins). It was not until 1862 that the US Treasury Department officially issued the first paper bills to make up for the shortage of coins and to fund the Civil War.

The present building of the First Congregational Church was rebuilt in a slightly different location in 1866 and cost just under eight thousand dollars. This, with its proud wooden spire was the most impressive of the three. Aged forty-nine, Jonathan Vickery became its very first preacher but, sadly, came to an untimely and hapless end five years later. He and a party of villagers went out in an open boat on a fishing trip. For some unknown reason the boat overturned and all were drowned. Mr Vickery left a very sad widow and seven children.

Then there was the United Methodist Church which was built in 1849 and stood proud with its elevated clock tower. Yes, it was made of wood and it was white.

The South Chatham Community Church was erected in 1911 and was a brick-built construction, but it burned to the ground six years later. I am not quite sure why it went up in smoke but I did hear of an unfounded rumour that the vicar was partial to a crafty late-night fag in the vestry. Personally, I think it was the work of the Almighty. My guess is he wasn't pleased with the choice of building material used and wanted it rebuilt in natural wood like everything else in this town. In 1919, after numerous money-raising ventures, that's exactly what the locals did. Then, when it was finished, some bloke walking past with his dog said, 'I've got a great idea! Let's paint it white!' And so it came to pass.

On our drive back to Orleans Deb noticed a turning at the last moment signposted Nauset Beach. In a screech of burning rubber I performed a Starsky and Hutch-like handbrake turn in the middle of the road and followed the narrow dirt path towards the shore. The reason for this reckless behaviour was due to last night's barman, who mentioned that there was a fantastic B&B near Nauset Beach called the Ship's Knees. I know, I didn't believe it was called that either.

We soon found it. For some reason the area infused me with the compulsion to jump from my seat, tie the car to a post and give it a drink of water. We poked our noses inside the *Knees* and were once more greeted with a conspicuous nautical-flavoured ambience. It was really just a posh shack, all very quaint and only ninety-five dollars per night. The room we were shown had a king-size bed. The dimensions could have accommodated me and Deb, her two sisters and her mother. Not that I'm in to that type of thing, you understand. It took up most of the bedroom, in fact.

I immediately booked the room for the following day, our last one on the Cape. I could cancel the Sunday at our Orleans hotel on our return, avoid clogging up my arteries with cheap cholesterol-laden sausages and save fifty-five dollars. Happy snappies! Bolstered with unexpected bouts of energy, we left the car where it was parked and took a two-mile bracing walk along the white sandy shore.

There was not much to see other than a flat calm sea and miles of empty beach but with the sun on our heads and the ocean breeze making us appear carefree and interesting we were more than happy. I collected a few unusual looking shells from the sand, as I always do at the seaside, and donated them to my wife as tokens of my undying love.

Further up the road we stopped at Fancy Farm where we bought ourselves two ham salad rolls the size of which I had never seen before and filled our wind-tanned faces. I don't know when, why or by whom this legislation was passed, but it appears that food always has to big here.

Opposite stood a house that bore a remarkable resemblance to the Bates Motel in the film Psycho. On closer inspection it was a shop that sold second-hand clothes. No shop in this area, I've discovered, is built like an archetypal shop. They all appear to be houses that have been converted for the purpose.

Anyway, we ventured in. It was dimly lit and smelled of very old people; a mustiness filled the air. Deb tried a few things on behind what looked like a shower curtain, which did nothing to appease my sense of foreboding, whilst I was left alone to be ogled by the three elderly ladies who ran the place. They were very chatty but in an uncomfortably prying, inbred sort of way. And their eyes! For the first time in my life I felt as if I was being undressed by members of the opposite sex all old enough to be my grandmother. Thankfully, nothing that Deb tried on fitted or took her fancy, so, after five uncomfortable minutes and feeling very relieved, we left.

'Did you hear a scratching sound coming from behind that locked door?' I asked Deb, as we got back in the car.

'No. It must be a cat or something,' Deb said, dismissively.

'Mmm! It's the *or something* part of that sentence that worries me,' I replied.

The remainder of the drive homeward was a touch surreal. My head was awash with visions of emaciated customers groaning and clawing their fingers to bloodied stumps behind that locked door; kept prisoner in order to gratify the wanton, sexual urges of three perverted old ladies. I could hear the captives' desperate pleas, all begging for freedom – or at least a cup of tea and a slice of Victoria sponge.

I shook my head as if it were an etch-a-sketch screen to expunge the whirligig of unsavoury images and turned on the car radio. The dulcet tones of Hank Williams singing Your Cheatin' Heart suffused the car. Once more, love and harmony filled my world.

A long and exacting day provided us with the fatigue necessary to be able to sleep like babies in our Orleans Inn bed for the last time.

~~

Whoa! We were woken up with seagulls screaming at the bedroom window. They appeared to be in a particularly agitated state. 'God, what a din,' said Deb, with a yawn, 'what's upset them?'

'I saw them hanging around the hotel's rubbish bins yesterday afternoon. I reckon they're complaining about those bloody sausages,' I said, closing the window.

After a bangerless breakfast, we checked out of the Orleans Hotel and drove to the Ship's Knees which I presumed was another seafaring term. We booked in to our room and immediately decided to take our marginal hangovers onto the beach.

Back in the room, I headed for my laptop. I've heard of knobbly knees, the bee's knees and *Knees up, Mother Brown* (which sounds very painful for the poor woman), but the Ship's Knees? So, I'm off to my great friend Google.

Ah! Just found out that the ship's knees are the curved pieces of wood used as a common form of bracing used in boat building. That's a shame, I was expecting it to have a far more exciting meaning. As I was in the mood, I searched for more sea-going body parts but the ship's nostrils, buttocks and bollocks, alas, were nowhere to be found.

Our last day here and this time we woke to the morning sun driving through the thin curtains hanging off our cabin wall. I can think of a lot worse ways to be roused from a good night's sleep. We ducked and swerved our way through the labyrinth of low-ceilinged corridors to our new breakfast room where dry waffles and blackcurrant jam awaited. The only other people in the room were a family of three – father, mother and their daughter who wore braces on her teeth. Thinking about it, nearly every young teenage girl I've encountered in this part of the world has braces on her teeth. 'What's wrong with slightly wonky Hampstead's?' I ask. Bit of character. American dentists must be raking it in.

The family were from Colorado and they were possessed of a slightly pompous aura that said we are deeply religious be careful what you say. I don't think they were particularly taken with my airy humour on Easter Monday. This day, I now know, after receiving a small lecture from Jackson, the circular father of the trio, is not celebrated as a religious festival and is not a national holiday in this country, but it wasn't long before the sermonising tone of his monotonous voice began to cause my waffles to turn up at the edges. I realised it was time to leave the Jackson Three to preach amongst themselves.

Big Brian, the proprietor of the establishment, had arms like Popeye and an enormous round face, which had a ruddy complexion that could have lit a fire. He seemed totally out of place running a B&B. He would have looked far more at home on a farm, up to his ship's knees in cow dung. Still, he was very friendly and more than accommodating when, after breakfast, he printed off our return trip home from his PC with the help of MapQuest.

After a five and a half hour return journey we headed for the gym to sweat away four days of excess from our abused bodies. When we weighed ourselves after our workout I was ten pounds heavier than when I arrived from England and Deb had grown seven pounds larger. Cripes! This was not good: time to take stock.

I am really looking forward to getting my tooth capped tomorrow; this temporary one is starting to rub me up the wrong way again.

Chapter Thirteen

There was an imposter camping in my mouth. The painful state of affairs was akin to having a size-nine foot wedged into a size-six shoe. My gum was red, sore and dominating my every waking moment. The only plus was that the sun was shining over this sleepless city so I took the opportunity to walk through Central Park once more on my way up to the dentist's surgery to get my new tooth.

On my arrival it was made abundantly clear that their main priority was not my comfort but the transference of monies. Whilst I was lying on my back beneath this beast of a woman, undergoing the new fitting, they rang Deb to get the card details in order to extract the princely sum of one thousand seven hundred dollars from her business account – a procedure that would have cost me in the region of two hundred pounds and the promise of a Christmas card back in GB. Hopefully, the company's insurance will cover the exorbitant cost.

After much grinding and reshaping, the tooth was stuck successfully in the pertinent gap, to be followed by a clean and polish. Shrek stood there looking very pleased with herself and her handiwork. I have to say, it did look pretty good in the small mirror that was held in front of my gaping mouth… but then, for one thousand seven hundred dollars, it should bloody well look fantastic, I thought, as I climbed out of the chair.

On the walk home I found myself smiling at everyone I passed hoping they would notice what a wonderful and comprehensive set of teeth I now had in my head.

Later, sat snug in front of our TV, we watched a comedy series called *Two and a Half Men* whilst eating fried chicken and three veg. My expensive tooth came through with flying colours and went on to be a firm and trusted companion, as did *Two and a Half Men*, which eventually sailed across to the UK with the same long-standing success.

~~

What a difference a day makes. Today, it rained throughout its duration, the highlight being a 1995 episode of Ground Force. The stark reality that I was holed up in a small flat with no friends to ring or visit hung over me once more like a wet blanket. As I peered out onto a sodden 2nd Avenue I was struck by the marked difference in my demeanour. Everything looks and feels so different in the rain, especially constant rain. The cars, trees, buildings and people all look a similar colour, as greyness washes over everything. There's a draining sense of negativity that muddies the senses when a tormented sky is gurgling yards above your head and all around is flat and uninspiring.

I watched the passers-by. They no longer strolled or walked; they struggled, dodged and scuttled. Theirs wasn't a journey to a destination – it was a competition. Shrubs and flowers appear weakened, uncomfortable beneath a persistent downpour, only gaining strength when the rain ceases and the sun breaks through... and we're the same.

You'd think I would be used to this weather, living in England, but I'm not and never will be.

~~

Rainy days seem to be few and far between in this place, thank goodness. The sky this morning was the best colour available and endless; the temperature pushing 60°F. My daily dose of Nut Crunch was becoming the breakfast equivalent of American TV; both pursuits leaving me with an innate sense of vacancy.

Boiled egg and soldiers! That's what I'll have. And I did, which was supplement enough to carry me up to 33rd and 8th and Penn Station. This was to suss out the train times for tomorrow's trip to Long Beach on Long Island. The name Long Island conjured up all manner of exotica in our minds. We had both been looking forward to this trip from the day we left England.

The subway steps took me down, not into a complex of small tunnels that I was expecting, but into a massive underground concourse. I was amazed to see the equivalent of Paddington Station hidden beneath the streets of Southwest Manhattan.

After a brief wander around and five minutes spent listening to a jazz trio delivering a few lively numbers to its preoccupied audience, I acquired a train timetable of the LIRR (Long Island Rail Road) and emerged back into brilliant warm sunshine. On my return journey I decided to take a walk back along the river, down 12th Avenue, Westside Highway for no other reason than I had not ventured that way before. Having done scant research of this area I had no idea what to expect.

I very soon chanced upon the New York Motor Show. Surprisingly, there was no admission charge, so I wandered in and found myself amid some very costly, ridiculously extravagant cars and beautiful old classic motors, but I have to confess that it's not really my bag, as they say over here.

As long as a car works and has a decent sound system – that'll do for me. The specifications of the greasy bits lurking beneath the bonnet leave me tepid at most. I carried on down towards the river. I soon spotted a jetty where a raft of posh passenger cruisers were birthed. I weaved a slow journey to the end of the boarded pier, taking in each aspect of the rows of stylish vessels that bobbed and strained against their moorings. When I could go no further I sat down on the rough wooden surface with my feet dangling a few yards above the flow. What is it about even a modest expanse of water that soothes the soul so effortlessly?

Once more, taking advantage of the wide open space in front of me I wrote this entry in my little notepad with the sun skipping a merry dance across the Hudson whilst gently braising the top of my head. The feeling of relaxation and sense of freedom when you find a location such as this in New York is immediate. As I left, I collected a brochure on dinner cruises. I plan to surprise Deb with one.

Further up the Hudson, I passed the Intrepid Air-Sea Museum. I didn't enter as I was more than content with my dose of exhibitions for the day, but I was mightily impressed by the monster of a US Navy aircraft carrier – the USS Intrepid – which sat motionless, too weighty to be rocked by a mere river, against the harbour wall. A collection of powerful looking fighter planes were sprayed around its capacious deck. The ship, I discovered later, served in World War II and was the recovery vessel for the Gemini and Mercury space missions.

Parked next to the battleship was the USS Growler, the oldest existing nuclear missile-carrying submarine – and it was enormous. For some reason the sight of a sub always gives me the shivers. I think it's that mysterious underwater thing; the dark depths that you can't see or trust. Just beyond this never ending expanse of grey metal was a plinth jutting out into the river on which stood the most fantastic piece of craftsmanship ever to take flight – Concorde.

It was the only aeroplane in modern history, when it soared over our heads, which made everyone look up in awe. That is some achievement. I never imagined that I could have regarded a plane with such majesty. It was beautiful. It first raced through our skies, piercing through our sound barrier on 12th March 1969. It was retired in late November 2003, three years after the Air France flight 4950 disaster, which saw this magnificent beast crash, shortly after take-off, killing all one hundred and nine people on board and four people on the ground.

The dwindling number of passengers, due to the lack of trust in the aircraft and the backlash of 9/11, plus Concorde simply being financially unviable, were the reasons given for its demise. As far as I know there are no plans to replace it, which I find awfully sad.

Some time later, when I met Deb after work, we stood beneath the most stunning sunset and decided we needed to get as near to the display as possible before it disappeared over the curve of our planet. With that in mind we thought we'd visit the Rainbow Room at the top of the Rockefeller Plaza. Alas, we were turned away due to me wearing jeans. Designer jeans at that. I come all this bloody way to visit a renowned landmark and get refused entry due to the material wrapped around the lower half of my body – incredible.

'I know,' said Deb, 'we can go up to the rooftop bar at the five-star Peninsular Hotel on 5th Avenue, between 55th and 56th. I've been there before. It's really impressive.'

Alas, it was closed for refurbishment. By this time, the moon was winning its tussle with the sun, pushing it steadily beyond a forest of skyscrapers. So, with only a fading navy blue canopy above us we had to settle for a couple of sherbets in Turtle Bar, a few blocks from our apartment. Ray, the barman, made up for our earlier loss by being a ray of sunshine himself. Not the same though.

We dined on pizzas the size of dustbin lids back in our condominium. Incidentally, I'm not particularly comfortable with that word "condominium": it sounds like the smallest size of Durex to me and what man would admit to wearing one of those?

~~

We're off to Long Beach. The temperature, so our radio told us, was meant to be pushing $70°F$ – nice timing. Showered and relaxed, we jumped in a taxi which managed to propel us forward one hundred and fifty yards in just over five minutes. I didn't expect the traffic to be so heavy on a Saturday morning. When we finally pulled up outside the station we had four minutes in which to buy two round trip (return) tickets and jump on our train. Sweaty and no longer relaxed we made it – just.

The train took us immediately beneath the East River emerging up onto Long Island. After a few minutes, having skirted Queens, we were trundling past tree-lined streets laced with houses that actually had gardens. The early sight of space and bold splashes of green again came as a welcome surprise. I could feel myself easing into the seat as we travelled south. The buildings shrank as the gaps got wider and nature began to reassert herself.

After another half hour, as we passed through Far Rockaway Station (great name – sounds like a James Taylor number), the views from our window were of brightly painted boats bobbing up and down in countless mini harbours that sat on meandering inland waterways. We were flashing past more expansive looking homes now but, whether large or small, I was amazed at how many people in the US have the American flag flying outside their homes.

Our British flag is a sight rarely seen in the UK and quite often associated with militant socialism. Why? I don't know, to be honest. To hang your national flag from your house in my country is regarded as rather naff, unless it's a really special occasion, such as winning the Football World Cup. Whereas the Yanks love giving a constant reminder to themselves and all the rest of us that they are American and proud of it. Although I quite like the design of the American flag, this public show of overt patriotism is all a bit too jingoistic for my more reserved and delicate English tastes.

We arrived at Long Beach station an hour after we left Manhattan and immediately headed for the beach. Our journey took us past a series of bungalows and two storey houses all with front porches like the one in *The Waltons*.

The closer we got to the shore the stronger the wind became and the promised seventy degrees didn't feel like seventy degrees at all. Long Beach had a boardwalk that stretched for as far as the eye could see. The worn wooded slats divided the interminable strip of sand from the rows upon rows of grey and muddy-brown, flat-fronted apartment blocks. Who or what built these eyesores?

My heart sank as this prosaic seaside resort did not even begin to approach my expectations. I was anticipating pretty, bougainvillea-covered seafront cottages, swaying palm trees, a sprinkling of luxurious hotels with extravagant swimming pools and toe-tickling white sand. None of the aforementioned treats were present and the beach was littered with cigarette butts, empty beer cans and broken bottles from, I'm guessing, drunken beach parties.

I know it was out of season and I may have been unlucky or just in the wrong part but it felt more like Long *Forgotten* Beach to me. After an hour of dodging cyclists and joggers along the boardwalk we took refuge from the cold breeze in the only beach-front cafe available, that went by the name of Why The Fuck Are You Here. Well, it may as well have been. Our presence amongst the drab plastic tables and chairs swelled the number of customers in the place to three and one of them was a dog.

But, I have to report that the hamburgers, fries and large coffees were not at all bad. The sustenance, served up by a pretty girl (yes, braces) not more than fifteen, along with her rotund and suspicious father, who was the chef, gave us the inner warmth needed to brave the weather once more.

The rest of the day, apart from watching a beach volleyball game, was disappointing, but it got us out of the city for a day.

When we arrived back, Penn Station was hot and sticky and alive with busy people. I've heard stories of how unhealthy the car fumes become and generally uncomfortable this city can get in the summer and with that in mind I'm glad we won't be here when it arrives.

~~

Central Park had transformed itself in the space of a week and was now unrecognisable. The trees and newly flowered shrubs that fringed the transaction of weaving pathways provided a welcome depth and range of colours to lift the soul. A sprawl of recumbent bodies filled the gentle slopes of the grounds and at certain places not a blade of grass could be seen.

Every few hundred yards or so there would be some form of entertainment on view. None of these amusements, as far as I knew, had been officially organised by the park authorities. These people just turned up and performed for the delectation of the passers-by or to receive a few dollars in a battered hat. There were roller skaters of all ages in a large, square roped-off area coasting and dancing to rap and heavy metal music; single musicians playing on instruments that ranged from guitars and bongos to penny whistles and a Chinese violin, which was played vertically. I'm not sure why, but it seemed to make sense that it should be played that way.

Further along, a group of black guys, their ages ranging from ten to late twenties, were tumbling and spinning on their backs to taped hip-hop music and very impressive it was too. The pick of the bunch for us was a skiffle/jazz band performing and singing old Cole Porter standards and other songs from that magical period of music.

It was impossible not to stroll around with smiles on our faces as couples, families and friends laughed and frolicked in the much awaited warm air amid the varied distractions.

I have to admit I'm not a great lover of crowds, but during the three hours we spent in this thoughtfully constructed sanctuary I never once had the inclination to be anywhere else in the world. I'll say this for the Yanks, they know how to chill out and how to party but, unlike the British, there is no sense of embarrassment or reticence to get up and do their thing.

We witnessed sights that on first appearance were frankly hilarious, outrageous or simply pathetic. By the time the sun had started to wind down my first impressions had completely altered. Why not dress up in what makes you feel good – whatever your age? All this horsing around was certainly not harming anyone. Who was I to say what is good or bad taste? I don't recall ever seeing so many happy faces together in one location. It was a revelation, but some did look rather ridiculous!

~~

As the balmy weather continued, most of the city's inhabitants were now dressed in floaty skirts and blouses, shorts and polo shirts. Everyone appeared to have slipped down a gear, bearing a more casual deportment as they traversed the warm sidewalks of a city emerging from its winter break.

I'm off to 5th and 42nd today. There sits another park in Manhattan that doesn't enjoy anywhere near the tranche of publicity afforded to its big brother, Central Park and I don't know why. Yes, it is considerably smaller, but the location is stuffed full of fascinating history, sculptured beauty and countless amenities. So, I feel I must share it with you.

In 1686, New York Colonial Governor Thomas Dongan designated an area, now known as Bryant Park, as public property. In 1822, the land came under the jurisdiction of New York City and was turned into a potter's field (burial site). This was decommissioned in 1840 in preparation for the construction of the Croton Reservoir. Opening two years later, it was a man-made four-acre lake enclosed by massive fifty-foot-high and twenty-five-foot-thick granite walls. Blimey! A bloody reservoir. Fort Knox doesn't have that much padding and security.

Despite this reckless use of igneous rock, the water supply system was deemed one of the greatest engineering triumphs of nineteenth-century America. It was an integral component of the first supply of fresh water carried by aqueducts into the city from upstate New York. Iron pipes transported the water over forty miles to the receiving reservoir in the area that is now Central Park, thence to the distributing Croton Reservoir. What a joy it must have been to be able to get clean drinking water simply from the turn of a tap – beats going down to the river with a rusty bucket.

Following the success of the Great Exhibition of 1851, held in the famed Crystal Palace exhibition hall in London's Hyde Park (later rebuilt at a site in Sydenham), a deeply impressed and mildly jealous New York City decided to replicate this event with their own version. So, the New York Crystal Palace was erected on Reservoir Square alongside the Croton Reservoir. The glass and metal structure was built in the shape of a Greek cross; the opening ceremony being on 14th July 1853.

Now here's a strange and creepy coincidence. The Sydenham and New York Crystal Palaces, each having experienced financial problems and periods of waning popularity, were both, can you believe, destroyed by fire. In 1858, the US version's blaze started in the lumber room, which I believe was a sort of store room. Within fifteen minutes the dome had crashed to the floor and after another ten the entire structure was a pile of broken glass and smouldering ashes.

In 1936, fifteen days after Bonfire Night, it was an explosion in the ladies cloakroom (the less said about that the better) that did for the UK building. Ninety fire engines and close to five hundred firemen failed to extinguish the raging inferno, fuelled by the old timber flooring and the high winds that were present that night. It burned for five hours reddening the faces of the huge watching crowds. And, so the reports state, the fire-glow in the sky could be seen from ships in the English Channel. Incredibly, no-one was killed in either catastrophe.

What do you think the odds would be of two sister structures, with exactly the same name but in countries three-and-a-half thousand miles apart, built predominantly of glass and steel, both perishing in accidental fires? Pretty long I'd guess.

I know what you're thinking – what's this got to do with Bryant Park? Well, it was in 1884 that Reservoir Square was renamed Bryant Park to honour the long-time editor of the New York Evening Post and civic reformer, William Cullen Bryant (1794-1878). The construction of the New York Public Library, which sits at the South East end of the park and expands its entire width, began in early 1902 and was completed by 1911. The huge, majestic building was built on a raised terrace and was second in size only to the Library of Congress in Washington DC.

The Beaux-Arts design was constructed from marble and included two stone lions guarding the entrance which were later nicknamed Patience and Fortitude by Mayor Fiorella LaGuardia – not my first choice of name for two ferocious beasts placed in the middle of a thriving city, I have to say. Fearsome and Dangerous would be a better fit, surely; Gnasher and Bonecrusher, still fairly appropriate; even Lenny and Clarence would be a slight improvement.

As I entered the building, my first emotion was one of reverence. I felt as if I was entering the state rooms of Buckingham Palace. One splendid hall followed another, boasting extravagant arches and voluminous cupolas, joined in a series of cadenced waves that rolled lazily over my head.

When I reached the main reading room I was blown away by the size and grandeur of this awe-inspiring chamber. It was as if I had slipped into aristocratic dreamland. The ninety-metre-long and twenty-five-metre wide book-lined walls were enough in themselves to make me feel rather insignificant, but the ornamental ceiling, which stood fifty feet above the endless rows of oak desks, was stunning in the extreme. The ornate canopy was embellished with maidens, cherubs and scowling satyr masks each casting their haughty gaze down upon my straining neck and dilated pupils. Again, I was immensely impressed by the architecture and attention to detail of one of Manhattan's iconic structures.

In 1934, architect Lusby Simpson was given the job of redesigning the park that had undergone many forced changes. Sorry, I just have to interrupt this story for a second. Do you know, I think it must be a prerequisite, if you want to become an architect, that you have to have a foppish or flamboyant sounding part of your name, or at least one that no-one has ever heard of before.

'I name this child Lusby Simpson.'

'My God!' you can hear the congregation gasp. 'He's going to be a bleedin' architect!'

Take a look at this list of just a handful of architects I have already mentioned in my story thus far: J Augustus Roebling; his son Washington Roebling; Henry Janeway Hardenburgh; William Burnet Tuthill; Frederick Law Olmstead; Calvert Vaux. See what I mean? Not a Fred Skinner amongst the lot of them.

Don't get me started on English architects. OK, just one then: Isambard Kingdom Brunel, born in 1806 in Portsmouth, whose father was sentenced to five years in a debtor's prison, but was released after three months due to some serious string-pulling. You can imagine how *his* name went down with the kids at school; not to mention his neighbours, made up of beer-swilling sailors, rough-arsed dockers, thieves and lipsticked prostitutes – all rife in this early nineteenth century location.

Anyway, back to good old Lusby. Having recovered from possible merciless teasing for most of his school life, he sat down with a large piece of paper, headed Bryant Park, and created a classical scheme of a large central lawn, formal pathways and meandering stone balustrades.

As I wandered through Lusbyland it was clear to me that a host of updated attractions had been added over the years. It was a delight to witness the many amenities and eye-catching images on show. Winter Village, in the centre of the park, consisted of a large ice rink surrounded by a glut of boutique-style holiday shops that sold anything from clothes to jewellery; decorative goods to local food. Elsewhere, there was a carousel, areas to play chess and backgammon, Bryant ping-pong, the Bryant Park Grill, sundry food kiosks and restaurants and I counted seven monuments dedicated to all manner of dignitaries and do-gooders.

One such commemoration, I feel I must mention, is the pink granite Josephine Shaw Lowell Memorial Fountain, which is not only a mouthful but was the first US public memorial dedicated to a woman. Josephine (1843-1905), who sadly lost her husband of one year in the American Civil War, dedicated her life to social justice, reform and the eradication of poverty. She went on to form the Charity Organization Society and the New York Consumers League, which strove to improve the conditions and wages of working women in New York City.

I think all that excellent work merits your own fountain, don't you?

I suppose the real joy of Bryant Park was just being amongst a swathe of happy-go-lucky folk meeting for lunch, having a stroll, listening to music or simply sitting on a bench reading a book.

I've just realised that I have devoted considerably more time telling you about Bryant Park than the world famous Central Park. Well, someone's got to stand up for the little guys.

In the evening, we poked our noses inside the Turtle Bay Grill and Lounge that Amy had recommended a few weeks back. The place was packed and absolutely rocking from its rafters. In fact, if it hadn't been attached to the ground it could easily have sashayed straight down 52nd Street, bounced across 1st Avenue and plunged straight into the East River.

In one corner, there were two guitarists playing and singing middle-of-the-road, country-flavoured covers and they were very good. I got speaking to them during their break and they invited me to play a few numbers. I took to the small stage and performed three songs to an appreciative crowd. I love the laid-back way the performers in this town encourage anyone who can bang out a half-decent song to get up and go for it.

The musician in me would love to stay in this city forever, where there are numerous bars providing live music in front of enthusiastic audiences. This practice, which is also very prominent in Ireland, has not been much embraced by England and I don't know why.

For some reason I hadn't been feeling too chipper for the past few days but tonight's experience got my ions positively crackling once more. Isn't it wonderful how just a small, seemingly insignificant but warm gesture can raise ones spirits from the lees at the bottom of your glass to the froth on the top of your pint.

My good friend Steve and his girlfriend Susan are arriving for a week's holiday next Sunday. I'm looking forward to seeing him and showing them around Manhattan.

Chapter Fourteen

Today, the allure of this capital was pulling me thirty-five streets south to check out The High Line, which is principally in the District of Chelsea and sits on the Westside of the Flatiron District; so-called after the building of the same name and derived from its apparent resemblance to a cast-iron clothes iron.

The stroll from my apartment was across Midtown and down to 20th Street and 10th Avenue and took just over half-an-hour. On the way I passed through the Flower District on 28th between 6th and 7th. This is Manhattan's equivalent of London's New Covent Garden Market minus the fruit and veg.

The street is lined with market stalls and rows of shops all selling plants and flowers imported from places as far away as Holland, South America and New Zealand. It has been in operation for over a hundred years and most of the original families, so I discovered later, were still in residence having passed the business down from each generation.

I weaved my way between exotic palms, bamboos and banana plants shipped in from the tropics. I swerved around stunning displays of multicoloured blooms ranging from peonies to pansies, lilies to lavender; all strutting their stuff from rows of wooden shelves and upturned metal buckets. I marvelled at the sprays of exquisite silk flowers that looked exactly like the real thing. As a matter of fact, most of them looked better than the real thing.

It really was like walking through a mini tropical forest, but without getting your shoes wet, and the smiling faces of the proprietors were a delight. The atmosphere was cool, relaxed and I soon realised that my footsteps were getting shorter and slower.

You see, it's the simple gifts that nature delivers to our door for free that soothe the troubled soul – a silent mist-shrouded lake; sun-dappled woodlands thronged with carpets of bluebells; a win on the lottery.

By way of a complete change of mood you may be interested to know that back in the mid-to-late 1800s, just before Coronation Street and before 6th Avenue became famous for all things horticultural, the area was known as Satan's Circus. The district was ripe with brothels, gambling dens, rampant crime, salacious saloons and all-night dance halls, where the sight of a drunken punch-up beneath a waning moon was as common as flared trousers in the '70s.

A few blocks further on I came face to face with the Flatiron Building, which was quite an extraordinary sight due to the perilously wafer thin composition of the structure. I was going to say it reminded me more of a Toblerone than an iron but it was nowhere near as sturdy as the chocolate bar. It was more akin to a thin wedge of wood that you would slide under a table leg to stop it wobbling. I was genuinely afraid for the workers within: I felt as if a rogue gust of wind could have sent it surfing all the way down 5th Avenue.

Walking swiftly past I finally made it to my destination – Chelsea. The neighbourhood was primarily residential; a mixture of tenements, towering apartment blocks and my favourites – townhouses. These attractive dwellings all had a set of steps, enclosed by black, painted railings, leading up to the front door. Most of these buildings in this area had red/brown fascias that I found warm and pleasing to the eye.

The area takes its name from the Georgian-style house and estate of the retired British soldier, Major Thomas Clarke. He obtained the area of land in 1970 and chose the name Chelsea after the Royal Chelsea Hospital and old soldiers' home, in honour of his comrades in London. The hospital stands today as an independent charity providing care and accommodation for veteran soldiers. The Chelsea Pensioners, as they are known, must have no dependent spouse or family to qualify as a resident.

The hospital was founded by King Charles II in 1682. A rather splendid, but camp, chase-me-Charlie, hand-on-the-hip bronzed statue of him stands in the central court of the complex. The reason for this whimsical swerve back to London was because I simply had to tell you the name of the statue's creator. Grinling Gibbons. See, I told you! Eccentric names are the preserve of the creative; the artists and designers of our world. There was no way this guy was going to be a postman, was there.

'Yes, young Grinling is showing great promise. We're moving him out of the sorting office next week, giving him a bag, a shiny cap and a bike (with clips) and letting him loose on the streets.'

No, not on your Nellie. Not for master Gibbons. He was destined, by virtue of his fancy moniker, to be wealthy, famous or both.

Right, enough of that... back to New York. What I had come to see was now stretched out above my head: the High Line. In the mid 1800s, trains used to run on street-level tracks down the Westside of Manhattan. For safety, the railroad hired men to ride horses and wave flags in front of the trains, but, after numerous accidents between freight trains and other sundry traffic on the many street railroad crossings, it wasn't long before 10th Avenue became known as Death Avenue.

It was decided, after what seems to me to be a rather long discussion, to build a raised track. The thirteen mile project opened to trains in 1934. Standing thirty feet above the ground it was designed to go through the centre of blocks, connecting directly to warehouses and factories. The trains, carrying anything from foodstuffs to raw and manufactured goods, were able to roll right inside the buildings to be unloaded without disturbing the street traffic. All very ingenious, but at one hundred and fifty million dollars (two billion dollars or so now), it was all very expensive.

As the trucking industry grew, it eventually led to a drop in rail traffic throughout the country. In the 1960s, the southernmost part of the track was demolished. The plan was to pull down the whole thing until, in 1999, two guys saw it not simply as miles of rusty, weed infested tracking but as a groundbreaking vision of beauty. They formed a non-profit organisation called Friends of the Highline and, after much lobbying to the government, raised over one hundred and sixty-seven million dollars for their project.

The section running from Gansevoort Street, in the meat packing district, up to 20th Street is now a one-mile-long linear park, would you believe. It has to be the skinniest, snakiest park in the world, but, in a city that needs any distraction from the endless, honking vehicles and dizzy buildings, it gets my vote. And do you know what? It works.

Five years ago, during a brief whistle-stop tour, I made a return visit to the highline, which has been extended up to 34th Street. I sat on one of the many benches stationed along the winding route and absorbed my surroundings. Pebble-dashed and smooth boarded walkways mixed freely with gravel-mulched shrub and flower beds – a great deal of the species being self-sown over the many early years of redundancy and neglect. It was a completely different feeling from Central Park. There, you could hide away from the buildings and the madness. On Highline Park you were stuck right in the middle of the industrial washing machine, but instead of bustling through, head down, this was a chance to sit and take it all in.

This refuge of calm appeared to float above the harsh reality of restless city life that crashed, banged and throbbed just ten yards below my feet. I would like to take this opportunity to congratulate Joshua David and Robert Hammond and their associates for their imagination and efforts to preserve and transform this unique feature for the delight of people such as me. It was a quite brilliant and brave idea.

In the afternoon I walked uptown to spend a couple of hours in Central Park by way of comparison. This place is becoming a bit of a must-have now – a snatched, daily dose of endless elbow-room and vegetation. The only worrying thing is that most of the park wardens now recognise me and I get the impression, by the way they cast their wary looks in my direction, that they think I'm homeless or a stalker of some kind. I always smile and wish them good day but, as I've mentioned before and with good reason, I don't trust anyone in this country who wears a uniform. Actually, that goes for a lot of countries.

~~

Sleep did not come easily last night. Deb and I lay awake until the early hours for some unknown reason listening to the perennial police-car sirens ricocheting off the walls of the city's high-rises. Five days without alcohol may be beneficial to certain organs of my body but it doesn't help the other vital lesser-known bits that are responsible for allowing me to enter an immediate and dream-filled slumber.

Today, I was going even further south. I jumped in a taxi and headed down to the Financial District on the southern tip of this inverted front-leg-of-a-horse-shaped island. Ten dollars later, I was walking through Battery Park, situated at the confluence of the Hudson and East River. It was so named due to the artillery batteries that were positioned there in the 17th century by the Dutch to defend their fledgling city of New Amsterdam.

I had read, with interest, in my recently purchased New York booklet, a brief synopsis of Castle Clinton – a circular sandstone fort that was built in anticipation of the war in 1812. The castle had a long and varied history, and I was looking forward to seeing it, but, apart from an old round wall and a cannon, there wasn't much else to excite me and, if I hadn't been looking for this 19th century stronghold, I could have easily passed it by.

The castle is perhaps best remembered as America's first immigration station (1855-1890), at where more than eight million people blew in off the ocean and onto these shores. From 1892 to 1954 a purpose-built immigration station on Ellis Island then took over the reigns as the gateway to further millions of wannabe Americans. Unfortunately, the wood-built structure lasted just five years before it was destroyed by fire. Shortly afterwards, a new and I must say rather attractive replacement was erected in the French Renaissance Revival style. The building was of red brick with limestone trim but the stars of the show were the spiked domed turrets that reminded me of World War I German military helmets.

There was a welcome – not always hearty – during the early years, awaiting those looking for a better life, who had journeyed in all manner of vessels from many parts of the world. Amongst others; Irish, German, English, Mexican, Polish, Russian, Chinese and Scandinavians all fled towards this enormous splodge of vacant land with high hopes, suffering a number of tragic fatalities along the way. Many succumbed to ill-health due to the exacting conditions of their trip. The bodies of those who perished, so the stories go, were simply tossed over the sides of the ships and into a watery grave.

On their arrival, many of the same nationalities stayed together, travelling to different parts of the country and setting up their own mini colonies where, understandably, they felt more comfortable with a shared language and a familiar set of customs.

And there I suppose, in a nutshell, you have America – relatively new, huge, diverse and, to a great extent, living up to the timeworn reputation of *numerous countries within a country*. The USA really is a curious mixed bag of occupants. I steal a wry smile whenever I hear the phrase *all American boy* because, even if he exists, I don't honestly know what that means.

I sat down on one of the many benches placed beside the fondly-tended flower beds lining Battery Promenade bathed in aqueous sunshine. In a reflective mood, I gazed out past the Statue of Liberty and across the sparkling stretch of Atlantic Ocean. I thought of the hordes of immigrants, who had travelled hundreds, sometimes thousands, of miles in rat-infested, stinking ships with appalling sanitary conditions, mostly undernourished, many diseased and dying.

I then tried to imagine the look on their faces the moment they saw the proud, torch-bearing Lady Liberty, representing Libertas the Roman Goddess of Freedom, rising up from the sea with the sight of their future homeland stretching out behind her. I can only speculate on the feelings of overwhelming relief and sheer elation that must have resonated through every expectant spirit.

Pensioners can sit and look at the sea for hours. I've seen them, slumped in royal blue and white striped deckchairs at Brighton and Eastbourne gazing out, in silent preoccupation, over the fading miles of their undulating memories. With this thought in mind and aware that I had been similarly roosted for over forty minutes, I sprung to my feet like a gambolling lamb and took my leave from the shore.

With that same bounce in my step I strode back up Broadway and hung a right into Wall Street. My journey down into this infamous financial centre took me past the New York

Stock Exchange, which is the largest equities-based exchange in the world. It immediately joined my list of inspirational and dramatically crafted American buildings. The facade was of ivory coloured stone with six proud and lengthy Roman-like pillars topped by a marble pediment. This country certainly knows how to do grand.

The New York Stock Exchange had a chequered history. The Wall Street Crash of 1929, known as Black Tuesday was the biggest in the history of the United States. The crash was thought to be brought about by the legacy of the Roaring Twenties. Driven by recovery from wartime devastation, this decade was a time of wealth and excess; where US agriculture was largely neglected. This led to the ten-year Great Depression affecting all western industrialised countries. During this time of austerity, construction came to a halt in many countries, farming suffered as crop prices fell by as much as sixty percent. Many other industries such as mining and logging were hit hard. Unemployment in the US rose to twenty-five percent and in some countries up to a third were out of work. The negative effects of the Great Depression lasted, in many countries, until the beginning of World War II.

But, as with most periods of hardship, the good times eventually return and here was the evidence of that in all her pristine pomp: the New York Stock Exchange. Still standing, still trading.

Feeling fortified after a quick sandwich and mug of tea, I cut around a few corners, with the smell of the sea in my nostrils, and once more found myself on a sheeny-cobbled street smack in the centre of the South Street Seaport District. The road had a parade of modern shops, restaurants and welcoming bars extending under F. D. Roosevelt Drive, which weighed heavy under a ceaseless cavalcade of traffic. Here, the new sat comfortably with the old.

This designated historic district boasts some of the oldest architecture in downtown Manhattan. Early preservation efforts focused on a block of character-swathed buildings built in 1811 and the acquisition of a varied collection of sailing ships from times of buckles and swash. With further and more recent conservation the entire Seaport neighbourhood now entices you back in time to New York's mid-nineteenth century. This provides the visitor with a flavour of what the commercial maritime trade was like in those far-off days. It was akin to being on a film set and I revelled in this city's efforts to doff their cap to historical values.

Then I spied a pier jutting out into the Hudson River. What is it about a pier that makes you want to walk to its apex even though you can see it contains little of real interest? Needless to say, I did exactly that. Halfway along, I almost tripped over a contortionist who was going through his sinew stretching act dressed in a rather fetching pillar-box red, skin-tight lurex body suit. A must for my spring wardrobe.

As this skin-and-bone collection of a man was tying himself up in an impressive sheep shank it put me in mind of those pinched animals that are twisted together from squeaky, inflated balloons. At one point he was just a medley of unconnected limbs and a shiny bald head sticking out from the middle of it all. This man, I quickly decided, would not need any outside assistance if he gave in to the temptation for oral sex.

The pier consisted mainly of more indoor/outdoor eateries and bars, all with a healthy compliment of patrons, and all with the beguiling view of the *Peking*. This was a four-masted, fully-rigged sailing ship that took its first dip in the early twentieth century. Further along the dockside was the *Pioneer*, an 1885 schooner. Both appeared to be in immaculate condition and were all part of the Seaport Museum. I tried to imagine what a thrilling sight those two beauties must have been when in full billowed sail, riding the wind, cutting through the ocean waves on their travels to far-off lands.

~~

The other day I was scanning my booklet on New York that I'd brought over from England and came upon a small chapter that went under the title of Facts You Didn't Know About Manhattan. There weren't that many listed in my pocket sized pamphlet and some of them I already knew, but it whetted my appetite. I transferred my fingers from page to key and proceeded to enjoy a small factual feast. Then I thought, why should I keep these little gems to myself? So, here are the facts I found most absorbing.

Washington Square Park, which lies in the neighbourhood of Greenwich Village, is known as the chess playing centre of the city. The north side of the park is where 5th Avenue starts its journey, running out of steam some seven miles later when it reaches the Harlem River. The surface of the recreation area is dominated by paving and open spaces but here's where it gets interesting. Lurking below the chess players, the dog walkers and picnic tables lay twenty odd thousand bodies. In

1797 the site was a burial ground for the poor and unknown and victims of the yellow fever epidemic that hit the USA in 1805. In addition, so the story goes, there was one public hanging on the site. Mmm! Not sure I would want to stroll through this park on a dark and windy night.

This is difficult to believe, but true – a one year permit for a hotdog stand in Central Park can cost as much as two hundred and eighty thousand dollars. I know the park gets busy but, blow me down, you would have to hand out a cargo ship-full of sausages, buns and fizzy drinks, spanning twelve months of changeable weather, to make it profitable. You would need to sell over seven hundred and fifty dollars' worth of merchandise a day just to break even. If you take into account days of rain, snow and freezing temperatures, that figure goes up alarmingly, but the traders stump it up so they must make a decent living from the sale of flaccid, processed-pork torpedoes – I have to say, they're not my favourite nutritional treat.

New York City subway musicians don't just turn up and start playing their instruments, like their English counterparts do on the London Underground. They actually go through a rigorous selection process. Many of these musicians have performed at such revered venues as the Carnegie Hall before plying their trade down amongst the subterranean commuters. So my advice is, don't waste your money going to expensive concerts wedged into cramped seats and where the performers are little specks in the distance; get yourself down to the New York underground. It's warm, dry and free.

Most of us are aware of Dick Whittington's declaration that the streets of London are paved with gold. Apparently, that is true of both London and New York. There is a man who mines the New York City sidewalk cracks for gold on a permanent basis and he can make as much as six hundred dollars in a week. His name is Raffi Stepanian, a forty-three year old local resident, who crawls around the pavements of Manhattan's diamond district for chips of gemstones and tiny pieces of gold which are thought to rub off the clothes and shoes of the jewellery workers. If you don't mind buggering your knees up, pick up your trowel and head down to London's Hatton Garden and start scraping.

Women may go topless in public as long as the act is not being used as a business. This law came about due to a court case concerning gender equality in 1992. The power of women in New York is such that the New York Court of Appeal ruled in favour of two women who were arrested for exposing their breasts in Rochester Park on the issue of equal rights. The argument was that if men were allowed to go bare-chested in public then so should women. As far as I'm concerned, I am all for women's rights.

And here are a few quickies for you:

There is a birth every 4.4 minutes and a death every 9.1 minutes in New York City. So, I guess following those statistics, that the population is growing quite rapidly.

On 28th November 2012, not a single murder, stabbing, shooting or, in fact, any incident of violent crime whatsoever was reported for the entire day. The first time in New York's known history that has happened.

New York has the largest Chinese population of any city outside of Asia and the highest population of Puerto Ricans of any city in the world. If that's the case, by my reckoning and experience, New York City must surely have the most bicycles in the world.

The Big Apple is a term coined by musicians. It was rumoured that when interviewed they would say 'There are many apples on the tree but there's only one big apple' – New York City was the premier place to perform. Others hold different opinions concerning the origin of the unusual moniker but I'm sticking with the musical one.

And finally...

Albert Einstein's eyeballs are stored in a safe-deposit box in a New Jersey bank vault. Well, why wouldn't they be?

~~

During a mid-afternoon stroll around the streets near to our apartment, we were drawn into Clancy's bar, which was heaving with noisy customers – surprising for the time of day. The reason for the unusually large gathering soon became evident. The Kentucky Derby was being shown on their wall-mounted TV. The annual event, which is always held on the first Saturday in May is known and advertised in the US as *The Most Exciting Two Minutes in Sport.* They have obviously never watched Eddie the Eagle Edwards shivering his socks off, shitting himself at the top of a ski jump, waiting to see if he was going to die a horrible death in front of a bloodthirsty, slavering audience.

'Would you two like a Mint Julep?' asked the barman.

'Not for me, I'm trying to give them up,' I replied, much to the chagrin of the enthusiastic steward. My weak effort at humour, as per usual, fell on stony ground. 'What, pray, is a Mint Julep?' I added.

His face lit up. 'It's the traditional race beverage – iced bourbon, mint and sugar syrup,' he told me with expectant arched eyebrows.

Well, how could I disappoint him? I turned to Deb. 'Julep?' I received an excited nod. So, with MJ's in hand we sat and watched the celebrated race to the background of whoops and hollers from the locals.

The highlight for me occurred when the race had been run. I was amazed to see, immediately after the winning horse had come to a standstill, a woman dressed as a jockey ride up to the clearly knackered steed and rider, whose eyes were the only thing visible on his mud-spattered face. She then produced a microphone and attempted to interview him, horse-to-horse.

The thing was, every time she got close enough with the mike one horse or the other would take a step backwards or veer away, as horses are prone to do. So, we ended up with a fractured conversation, similar to our much-loved English comedian Norman Collier when performing his faulty mike routine. It was both hilarious and bizarre in equal measure.

Then they interviewed the winning owner, who was in a wheelchair and wired-up to breathing apparatus. Honestly! He was so thrilled I thought he was going to die there and then. I know I shouldn't have laughed...

Two Mint Juleps and all this excitement was more than enough for one day – with a nod to the barman, we retired gracefully.

Chapter Fifteen

'Oh, God! Chris.' The three words hit my ears in the form of a shriek. It came from the kitchen.

I rushed in from the bathroom, underpants on, toothbrush in mouth, and gurgled, 'What's up?'

Deb pointed at the toaster. I looked and frowned. I was just on the point of asking her why she was frightened of the toaster when two cockroaches appeared from behind the gleaming appliance. Deb jumped back two paces and I said 'Urgh!' and failed to squash either of them with the bread board before they legged it behind the cooker. Not my favourite insects and definitely not a good sign.

'Right, we must remember to keep all our food locked away in cupboards until I get this sorted with the agents,' I said to a now empty room.

The little buggers are really fast on their feet, all six of them. Apparently, these creatures can survive without food for over a month and are deemed to be the hardiest insect in the world. I read somewhere that if a massive nuclear war destroyed all life on this planet the cockroach would most likely survive. Don't you find that scary?

It was Sunday 2nd May and less than two weeks to our departure. Steve and Susan were arriving today into JFK at twelve thirty p.m. I can't wait to see them both.

The rest of the day was spent in the apartment; Deb writing letters to her family; me thinking of tunes to play on the guitar that would lure the roaches out of their lair. Nothing worked. Despite keeping a constant vigil and a rolled-up newspaper next to me for most of the day, the critters kept their heads down.

We met Steve and Susan at six thirty p.m. and caught up on what we had all been doing for the past ten weeks. The night ended in Mimi's, entertainment provided by Hunter Blue, our over-the-top, gregarious, gay piano player. He welcomed our guests very amusingly and publicly with an announcement fit for a celebrity duo followed by another flamboyant rendition of the British national anthem. By nine o'clock, Steve and Susan were hopeless victims of the dreaded jetlag. We arranged to meet them tomorrow evening.

~~

Our friends have brought the awful English weather over with them. It's dull, drizzly and... well, English. I was going to the gym today but I couldn't dredge up the enthusiasm to venture outside my apartment so me and the cockroaches stayed put in our warm and dry retreat. I had a workout in my sitting room; the roaches kept fit scuttling around behind the kitchen cabinets. I finished my exercises by running up our building's stairs to the tenth floor which, I must admit, almost killed me. I don't understand it: twenty years ago, I could run up ten flights of stairs two at a time before my heart even thought of knocking on my ribs. It had to be those damn Mint Juleps. What kind of name is that for a drink, anyway? Just to prove I was not old and past it I repeated the stair drill, which did kill me. I am now writing this posthumously.

We hooked up again with Steve and Susan in PJ Clarke's by way of a pre-dinner drink and to show off to them that the barman knew us by name. After two beers we climbed into a taxi (it was now raining again) to go to Tao the celebrated Thai restaurant that Deb and I visited a few months back.

I felt confident our guests would be as impressed with this venue as we were. Like us, they were taken aback; their faces lighting up like the rear end of fireflies. Despite having to wait forty-five minutes for our pre-booked table, the evening was a success.

~~

I recommended some of my favourite places to visit before Steve and Susan went gallivanting around Manhattan today. They kindly invited me along but I think it's much more fun to explore and discover new places without some smart arse, who has done it all before, giving you a running commentary. We arranged to see them tomorrow.

Deb went to work and I suddenly had the urge to visit theatre-land.

Running the breadth of lower Midtown Manhattan is 42nd Street, incorporating the previously visited Grand Central Station and Times Square. I had only walked through this area before by way of going somewhere else and as it was possibly the most written about part of this city I felt a touch remiss that I had not absorbed more of its attractions and history.

Turning right off 2nd Avenue, I was confronted with the sight that never fails to make me say, 'Wow.' Between 3rd and Lexington sits what I deem to be the finest structure in New York City – the marvellous Chrysler Building. A classic example of Art Deco architecture, the construction commenced in 1928. Two years later it was the completed headquarters of the Chrysler Corporation until the mid-1950s.

Surprisingly, it was never owned or paid for by the corporation. Walter P Chrysler decided to dip into his own bottomless pocket by way of an inheritance for his children. Thanks, Dad. But the Chrysler kids, needing the money I guess, sold it in 1953. Since then the ownership has changed hands numerous times. The last I heard it was owned by the Abu Dhabi Investment Council, as if they needed to make more money.

The corner ornamentation on the 31st floor are replicas of the 1929 Chrysler radiator caps. The silvery metal terraced crown, surely the most spectacular part of the building, reminds me of a handsome version of a barracuda with its flashing platinum scales and powerful head. Topped with a one hundred and twenty-five-foot spire, it may not be the tallest building in New York, but I think it stands head and shoulders above any other building that I have seen in this town.

The bulk of the theatres and cinemas are situated in and around Times Square which sits at the junction of 42nd and Broadway. Incidentally, Broadway is the only avenue that is not a completely vertical line. It starts straight, in Uptown Manhattan, then cuts down across the belly-button of the city from left to right like a bold scar. It returns to the perpendicular once more at East Village, and manages to reach further south than any of its contemporaries, finally running out of real estate at Battery Park.

This bustling centre of blatant vitality with its stonking great flashing neon signs, now frequented by tourists and the well-to-do, was a very different animal in the mid 20th century. From 1950 to the late 1980s, this was an area of sleaze, drug dealers, pickpockets, prostitutes of both genders and cinemas, which catered for every sexual proclivity.

It was only as recent as the early 1990s that the government oversaw a clean-up of the Times Square area. It is now a safe and lively location filled with mainstream theatres and movie houses and possessed of an incredible energy. It's worth a visit.

Tonight we dined at home and retired early as Deb is off again on a flying business trip to Toronto tomorrow morning. I just hope that she isn't strip-searched and treated as a threat to the safety of America again.

~~

I waved goodbye to Deb at five thirty a.m. as she climbed into a taxi waiting to whisk her off to the airport. After the shenanigans surrounding her last trip I was, understandably, concerned for her welfare.

Steve and Susan were taking a helicopter around this little island this morning. Good luck to them. I'm not a great lover of helicopters and New York has a worrying history of chopper crashes. In fact, a year after our stay two such helicopters, which took off from the same spot as my friends, both went down in the Hudson River within a week of each other. Fortunately, all passengers survived the terrifying experience. Despite being treated to a free and unexpected swim, they were not at all happy.

I brought my golf clubs out here with me and after eleven weeks of my twelve week stay I was finally going to get to swing them. Deb was in Toronto and doesn't play golf so I booked up to play with my visiting friends at the Bethpage Black course. This was where the 2002 US Open championship was played

Safe from their chopper ride, we loaded up the rental car and set off on the thirty mile journey to Farmingdale, Long Island. Apart from a few traffic problems our one hour journey from Manhattan was pleasantly unhindered.

As we proceeded up the long, swanky drive and into the enormous car-park I was very much taken with the neat layout and attractive clubhouse. The golf courses, there are five of them, have the names black, red, blue, yellow and green – I know, how do they think these names up – were constructed in the early 1930s and opened to the public in 1935. The black course was built with a championship layout and is rated as one of the most difficult in the country. Why were we playing the Black course, I hear you ask? Because we were allowed to and because we could dine out on it for years afterwards. Big mistake!

All five are public courses, which anyone can play, and the Black course was the first public course to stage the US Open. In Britain and the United States most championship courses operated on a private membership only basis so today was special indeed.

On the first tee, a Chinese American guy approached us and asked if he could join our threesome.

'Of course,' I replied. 'What's your name?'

I needn't have asked. It was Jim. All Chinese American blokes are obviously called Jim.

Just before we teed off, I noticed a sign. It read: THE BLACK COURSE IS AN EXTREMELY DIFFICULT COURSE WHICH WE RECOMMEND ONLY FOR HIGHLY SKILLED GOLFERS... AND YOU THREE ARE DEFINITELY NOT IN THIS CATEGORY. It didn't say the last bit, but it should have.

I've got kipper ties hanging in my wardrobe that are wider than some of the fairways. The greens are like postage stamps and there are voluminous bunkers in every direction to where my ball insisted on disappearing. In fact, there's far less sand on Bournemouth beach than on this vicious piece of soft landscaping.

In addition, the "rolling hills" aren't rolling at all; they are steep, tiring and difficult to negotiate. I can't possibly describe how useless this course made me feel as a golfer and a human being. I know Steve felt the same and it was Susan's very first game! God knows what she thought of her new sport. The last I heard she was still in therapy.

The round was hard on all of us, but poor old Jim only lasted till the fourteenth hole. After a swift look at his watch and with no other comment than 'Thank you, but I must go,' he dragged his little body, followed by his enormous golf bag, over a nearby rolling hill and disappeared out of sight.

We looked at each other in stunned silence, which was all we could manage in the circumstances. Whether it was the challenging course or the three useless individuals he had got stuck with that had made him decide he'd had enough, we can only hazard a guess.

Putting out on the eighteenth green, soaked in sweat, knackered, beaten, I wondered if this exercise in self-flagellation had been worth the enormous effort. Gradually, as we rested on the veranda, sipping our iced lemonades, shaded from the hot sun by a large and welcome cream parasol, a small shred of comfort began to emerge from my battered spirit. It was the realisation that we had just walked and played on the same haloed turf as the very finest golfers in the world. Exhausted but slightly smug we dragged our golf bags to the car and drove the slow, traffic-filled distance back to Manhattan.

My fears for Deb's safety were allayed on my arrival back home as she had returned early evening unmolested by uniforms.

After a shower and a face full of Aftersun we met up again with Steve and Susan at nine p.m., along with Amy and Ryan at the renowned Wolfgang's Steakhouse on 33rd and Park Avenue. Amy had made the booking and told them that she worked for a wine magazine. This resulted in us getting the best table in the house and being fussed over throughout our very expensive but delicious meal.

Despite strapping two iced beers to my cheeks, my face, as the evening progressed, was becoming reminiscent of a slapped arse and just as uncomfortable, but at least it was a great source of entertainment to all present at the table throughout the evening.

~~

Steve phoned today and announced that he and Susan were treating me and Deb to a World Yacht dinner cruise tonight. My first thought was would we have enough time to sail around the world and get Deb back to work on Monday morning?

At seven p.m., we met up at Pier 81 on West 41st Street in Midtown. All dressed in best bib and tucker we boarded the grand, snowy-white, three-storey yacht ready for our World Cruise. From our table, next to one of the many windows on the second floor restaurant area, we were able to observe the mighty New York City from a totally different perspective.

Our three hour dinner cruise took us down the Hudson, passing The Empire State Building and the eerie site of the once magnificent World Trade Center buildings. We then hung a left and swung around the tip of Manhattan, covered by Battery Park and South Street Seaport, where we glided past Governor's Island to our right.

This one hundred and seventy-two-acre isle was originally named Nutten Island by the Native Americans probably due to the plentiful hickory, chestnut and oak trees present unless, of course, there were no trees at all and there was nutten to see. (Sorry, couldn't resist it). In 1784 it was renamed when the British Colonial Assembly reserved the island for the exclusive use of New York's royal governors.

The sun was now beginning to lose its power, transforming the interesting to the spectacular. Manhattan, in a matter of minutes, had become a horizontal cluster of sparkling jewels, tiptoeing out across the water in reflections of gold and silver as our smooth running vessel now led us up the East River. Soon we were coasting serenely beneath the Brooklyn Bridge – the wonderful and theatrical lady, who three months ago, introduced us to this amazing metropolis.

Our outward journey stopped a few ripples short of the headquarters of the United Nations – a complex of mainly uninspiring buildings that has served as the official centre of the United Nations since its completion in 1952. The main office tower stands as close to the river as is possible without getting wet and looks like a giant cigarette packet. But the interior of the General Assembly Hall that sits alongside (I have only seen pictures to confirm this) is an absolute stunner. With its towering domed ceiling, inset with a myriad of subtle lights, it has the aura of an enormous spaceship; not dissimilar to the craft that shot off in a flash of neon leaving poor little, stiff-necked ET behind to fend for himself.

The boat then took us around the dramatically lit Statue of Liberty, where we were all summoned up on deck to marvel at the symbol of American freedom. The vessel continued on past Ellis Island and finally back to where we began.

During our thoroughly enjoyable voyage, we were treated to a pleasant four-course meal accompanied by the tasteful sounds of the on-board DJ. This was only after experiencing the oddest waitressing antics I have ever encountered. When this young lady first approached our table she started the evening in the widely accepted practice of taking the drinks orders, but, after she had asked Steve, Susan and Deb for their choice of beverage, she walked off. I was left open-mouthed and in a state of confusion whilst my wife and friends just guffawed. When she returned with the three glasses of cool refreshments, I said, as politely as the situation allowed, 'Excuse me, I haven't got a drink.'

'OK! What can I get you?' she drawled, as if it was I who'd forgotten to ask for one. I suppose an *Oops, I'm sorry sir,* is out of the question, I thought, as I ordered a beer. Honestly!

Now, whether I had discovered the secret of temporary invisibility or not I can't say, but incredibly she did the exact same thing when taking our food orders. The other three thought this hilarious. Was this girl not the full ticket? Did she suffer from myopia? Could she only count up to three? Maybe she just didn't like the look of me?

'Excuse me!' I called after her as she wandered from the table. No response... apart from four people looking over quizzically from the next table. 'Hello, waitress!' I tried again, a good bit louder. Now everyone else on the boat turned around apart from the bird-brain wearing the pinny. Still nothing. 'You there, with three orders!' I added in a shout.

By now, Steven, Susan and Deb were rocking in their seats, crying with laughter. Finally, she turned and looked back at me.

'How many people, would you say, are sitting at this table?' I said, trying to sound ironic.

''Scuse me?' she asked, as she returned.

'It's just that I thought it might be nice to join my friends and partake in some food as well. If that's OK with you?' I said, hopefully.

'Jeez! I'm not doing very well tonight, am I?' she replied, sheepishly.

'No!' I agreed. Then I realised: she wasn't any of the above, she simply inhabited a world that the rest of us pass into the moment we lose consciousness.

As it turned out, the farcical episode set the tone for the evening and we giggled our way around the nether regions of New York and all the way back to shore, which we reached safely by ten p.m. And that was that, really; another day of education done and dusted in New York, New York.

~~

Steve and Susan flew home this morning and we had an easy day. We took a random, leisurely walk in the morning, watched the DVD, Girl with a Pearl Earring, in the afternoon and although it seemed to be a good film, my mind was wandering throughout.

I've come to realise that spending three months in another country messes with the senses somewhat. Throughout my life, every time I have left my home for more than a few days it was to go on holiday. So, on our arrival here it was natural for part of my brain to click into relaxed vacation mode. But this is where it gets confusing because another part knows that I am not on holiday but here to live – to support my wife, integrate with my surroundings and the people within.

The trouble is, it is only a temporary arrangement. Therefore, the feeling of belonging and attachment, of being grounded, is rather elusive and, in my periods of solitude, of which there were many, I had the sense of being in a permanent state of transition. Not necessarily an unpleasant experience, just a little strange – a bit uncuddly.

Chapter Sixteen

There are now only four more days till we return to the island of my birth. I have been looking forward to it for the last week but today, surprisingly, I was feeling a touch nostalgic about the old place that refuses to have a kip. It suddenly dawned on me that I was going to miss this animated, heavy-breathing city when I am back in sleepy Surrey.

Tom, Deb's director boss, was over from England and I had arranged to meet him and Deb in PJ Clarke's after the working day. Shortly after six p.m., Tom and I were clinking glasses filled with Guinness, whilst I recounted some of the many odd and humorous incidents that had befallen me and Deb during our business trip to this stimulating madhouse.

During the pub dinner her boss, pre-armed with a mouth-full of flattering compliments concerning her achievements in the New York office, released them at carefully planned intervals.

'Thank you, Tom. I am thrilled you think so,' my wife said, looking proud and embarrassed at the same time. I could see she was genuinely chuffed.

Tom is one of those guys who, on first meeting, appears to be an amiable but business-like and generally measured man. But, after a few pints, there's an excitable little boy, full of fun and mischief ready to jump out from his directorial skin and say boo. I really enjoyed his company but took the opportunity to tell him how cheap he was getting Deb's services. He laughed it off but I think he may just have agreed with me.

~~

I dragged myself to the gym this morning and sweated buckets. This was the hottest day we've had here so far and the most humid. I was warned that the New York winters were harsh and the summers hot and sultry and I can attest to both. We are going home at just the right time as me and humidity are not the best of friends. Back home we will catch the last few weeks of our gorgeous, verdant spring and live in hope for a pleasant summer.

Last night we experienced a massive thunder storm with flashes of lightening illuminating the bedroom as if it was Guy Fawkes Night. I didn't sleep well, but then what's new in our NY apartment. Deb, as usual, maintained her uninterrupted programme of pleasant dreams despite the explosions of electrically charged particles going off outside our window. How does she do that?

The Americans, of course, don't celebrate Firework Night as we kids used to call it, but then they are veritably spoilt with numerous annual celebrations of their own. Apart from the obvious; Easter, Christmas and New Year, there's the Fourth of July – the 1776 signing of the Declaration of Independence and all of the following have their very own allotted Day: Veterans, Colombus, Memorial, Labor, Martin Luther King, Valentine's and President's. And don't forget Halloween. I think that's more than enough occasions for American man to get his rocket out and dangle his Catherine wheels from the nearest tree.

The last time I visited the Rockefeller Center, I was so captivated with the colourful flags, ice-skating rink, imperious statues and the cloud-parting GE Building that I virtually ignored the widely celebrated St. Patrick's Cathedral that stands opposite. Why? I don't know, because this Neo-Gothic style Roman Catholic Church was an absolute beauty and this is where I stood now.

Built in 1878, the huge proportions of this prominent landmark dominate midtown New York in a way that is so utterly disparate from the majority of its forgettable neighbours. The magnolia stone and marble frontage is impressively fussy – the stars of the show being a pair of slender, sharp spires that stab the heavens one hundred metres above the ground. As I passed through the arched entrance I was met by an avenue of massive stone pillars standing like sturdy oaks leading me down the aisle, through to the carpeted steps and up to the breathtaking altar encompassed by a cluster of sapphire-blue stained-glass windows.

I am not sure many of us, me included, really appreciate the role that churches and cathedrals played throughout the world in the Middle Ages. They were not merely retreats from the bustle of everyday life and a place to have a hurried word with the Lord as they are today. They were the focal point in the lives of the community. Victory celebrations, festivals, funerals, public meetings and feast days were just some of the countless reasons that townspeople flocked to their local places of worship.

St Patrick's Cathedral could also boast of having its share of recent notoriety. The requiem masses of such noted individuals such as Babe Ruth, Ed Sullivan and Robert F. Kennedy and the memorial mass of Andy (fifteen minutes of fame) Warhol were all held there. It was also the location used in many films such as Gremlins 2 and Beneath the Planet of the Apes.

I'm not sure the designer James Renwick, or the Almighty, Himself, envisaged their dazzling creation to be used as a meeting place for a bunch of crazed monkeys and big-eared, killer-goblins, but one has to move with the times, I suppose.

~~

Today is Thursday 13th May. The temperature was nudging eighty-five degrees and you could cut the atmosphere with a butter knife – it was steamier than Last Tango in Paris. It has taken three months for the letting agents to silence the pounding central heating pipes and, irony of ironies, we don't bloody need them now. The climate has now undergone a complete shift into oppressive rain-forest mode. The air is thick with car fumes and cooking smells that seem unable to detach themselves from the pavements of this industrious city. At least I don't have to go to the gym to sweat out the many impurities that have taken temporary residence in my system – walking to the paper shop does the job nicely.

I packed our extra bag that one of the directors had kindly agreed to take home for us and taxied it up to Deb's office. Luckily, the security guard didn't ask me to empty the contents out on to his desk. I took the lift up to the 52nd floor and entered her workplace in the clouds. All the staff then congregated in the boardroom where they presented Deb with a cake and a leaving present.

After a few speeches, all complimentary, all flattering, I was suddenly aware that I was surrounded by a lot of damp eyes. The house plants that Deb had wanted to introduce into the stark, unfriendly office had arrived that morning and so had a sense of camaraderie and order that was not present on our arrival here. Desks had been rearranged and tidied and drawers closed. Unexpectedly, I was filled with a chest-full of pride for my little English missus who by now also had tears streaming down her face.

I hadn't expected such an emotional farewell. I was going to miss this place and I'd like to think this office was going to miss my wife. I hoped the legacy she was leaving behind would retain a good measure of staying power.

I took a still tearful Deb back to the apartment where we attempted to fit everything we brought out from England, plus the stuff we had accumulated, into our groaning suitcases. In the evening we popped in for a quick drink at TJ Whitney's. Ronan, the barman, who also worked for The Irish Voice newspaper in New York, wanted a copy of a poem I had written about Central Park to publish in his journal. It would be nice to think that maybe I too could leave a tiny legacy in this great city.

~~

Going home day. The weather was a little kinder this morning as we strolled up to have a last look around Central Park. As far as I was concerned, this fine arena had indeed been central to my enjoyment, my relaxation and, most of all, my sanity. I was about to say goodbye to this whirling eddy of scuttling bodies, traffic-strangled but arrow-straight thoroughfares and the battalion of buildings that didn't just scrape the sky, they held rule over it.

We managed to secure, for the first time in three months, a seat in the conservatory of the Loeb Boathouse. This multi-windowed restaurant sat beneath an assembly of luminescent, aquamarine roofs and overlooked a placid boating-lake. The wood-built structure was badly in need of repair in the early 1950s but to its rescue came investment banker and philanthropist Carl Loebe, who dug deep into his pocket and pulled out three hundred and five thousand dollars that went to create the inviting structure we now found ourselves in. The restaurant was one long room that ran just short of the entire width of the lake affording every table an uninterrupted view of the glassy water and surrounding abundance of flowering shrubs and trees.

As we sat, peering outwards onto burgeoning spring, we reflected on our thirteen-week stay here. The conclusion was that we were both heartened with Deb's achievement in helping to transform an irresolute office sales team into a happy and focused workforce. But more so, we bathed in the thought of how lucky we were to be given an opportunity such as this; a funded trip to one of the most exciting cities in the world. A chance to view a foreign country as an insider instead of the usual two-week holiday snapshot.

As we made our way through the bustle of Manhattan and back to our apartment to finish packing, my thoughts turned to England. The promise of sitting in a lush-green garden in fluffy Surrey was very appealing. The comfort and security of having my own home and possessions around me filled me with a warm sense of belonging. It was the country in which I was made – the place I loved.

But like anything in our lives, appreciation is greatly increased with comparative knowledge. This trip had strengthened how I valued my own country not because New York was, in anyway, inferior or less enjoyable. It was simply different. A magnificent animal in its own right. And, yes, this iconic city did live up to its celebrated reputation portrayed in countless nostalgic songs, books, musicals and films.

Gerard Kenny sang about, '... all the scandal and the vice,' and, as I have found out, this island has it in droves. But it's Frank's immortal words, 'I wanna be a part of it, New York, New York,' that best reflects the feelings I'm taking away. Because New York is now a part of me.

As England is calling me home I look forward to having two feet planted back on familiar soil and a happy and victorious wife by my side. In addition, I will have a much-probed and cherished overseas mistress tucked away in my heart, and I won't even have to feel guilty.